Praise for *Flying in tl*

"In a world crammed full of leadership books written by academic theorists whose faddish formulas become obsolete soon after publication, my friend, mentor, and real-life superhero Kim Campbell shares battle-tested, irrefutable truths that will never be obsolete! As a legendary fighter pilot, senior military officer, and university instructor, Kim reminds us that under pressure we don't rise to the occasion; we fall to the level of our training. Kim doesn't just teach what she knows—she teaches who she is, how she lives, what she's done—to illuminate the military mindset that makes leadership automatic. Being hit a hundred times in a combat mission over Iraq, and losing her high-tech hydraulic controls, Kim was forced to fly in 'Manual Reversion,' becoming an expert eyewitness that leadership will always be an analog job in a digital world! This is a must-read motivational masterpiece and behavioral bible for every entrepreneur, business owner, corporate executive, sports team coach, military leader, and civic influencer in the world!"
—**Dan Clark,** Hall of Fame Speaker and author, *The Art of Significance*

"I've had the distinct honor to serve with Kim Campbell while we were both on active duty in the United States Air Force, and now in the public business sector. When it comes to leading people and complex organizations, this exceptional warrior-leader truly 'walks the talk,' and is as good as I've seen in my 48-year professional career! In this engaging book, Kim really nailed it! She has delivered an invaluable resource for any leader's library . . . easy to read with incredibly relevant personal stories that are humble, interesting, and inspiring. Most importantly, Kim has done a phenomenal job of drawing out the 'so-what' lessons learned from her 'life experiences.' I suggest this book as a must-read for our Airmen during their professional military education courses, as well as for the public business leaders who want to drive a healthy organizational climate and culture!"
—**Robin Rand,** General, U.S. Air Force (Retired), Former Commander, Air Force Global Strike Command

"I need to warn you about *Flying in the Face of Fear*. Yes, start the book by reading the Prologue . . . but be prepared to get hopelessly hooked. Immediately.

Colonel Campbell is a master storyteller, and her own story is the stuff of legend. You'll see from the very beginning that this book is exceptionally gripping, intelligent, and filled with gold-standard advice for all leaders, all teams. Whether your personal military experience is extensive or nonexistent, this book is, quite simply, a great read . . . filled with clear and practical advice.

When Colonel Campbell spoke to our graduating seniors at their Commencement ceremonies, they—and all others in attendance—were absolutely in awe of her and her inspirational competence and courage. The students called her 'the real deal.' Indeed, she is.

Of all the books, dissertations, journal articles, and essays I have read and studied on leadership, team building, continuous improvement, and the like over the years, *Flying in the Face of Fear* is the most readable, the most accessible, and certainly the most compelling on a very personal level.

Thank you, KC, for giving the world this amazing and helpful account detailing your style of leadership, mentorship, and service. Everyone who reads it will be inspired to discover and nurture their own true courage."
—**Dr. Tiffany M. Franks,** President of Averett University,
  Danville, Virginia

"An absolute must-read for current leaders and aspirational leaders alike. Kim draws upon her distinguished career as a U.S. Air Force Academy graduate, decorated combat fighter pilot, and senior military command officer. By leveraging these exceptional experiences, Kim offers keen insights on leadership; lessons both learned and earned.

Kim's key messages on developing and leading high-performing teams, built on trust and bonded by a deeply held common purpose, should resonate with readers and be recognized as widely applicable. Examining leadership at its finest, Kim also emphasizes the human element: facing fears, being approachable, listening to your team, and humbly committing to continually learn while helping others along their own paths. Truly inspirational!"
—**Jeff Boyer,** Vice President, General Motors (Retired)

"Kim 'KC' Campbell is a fighter pilot's fighter pilot. She has seen and experienced it all . . . from sitting behind a desk . . . to training the way we fight . . . and ultimately going to war. Her words in this book jump out; the reader can feel her complete range of emotions. What is extraordinary in this book is how KC can take her unique military leadership lessons and provide insights to corporations to make them operate at a higher level. The United States Air Force was better because KC was a part of it, and now the rest of our nation can benefit from her wisdom."
—**Lori Robinson,** General, U.S. Air Force (Retired), Former
    Commander, United States Northern Command and North
    American Aerospace Defense Command

"Fighter pilot Kim 'KC' Campbell has delivered a gripping testament to the power of facing fear and embracing failure as a pathway to success. Aspiring leaders at all levels and from all walks of life will find inspiration in her stories of leading with courage to achieve victory over personal and professional challenges. This is a book that merits a place on every leader's shelf."
—**Sandra Stosz,** Vice Admiral, U.S. Coast Guard (Retired) and author
    of *Breaking Ice & Breaking Glass: Leading in Uncharted Waters*

"*Flying in the Face of Fear* is an exciting story about leading with courage and humility. Whether leading a small team or a major corporation, all leaders can learn from KC's lessons on vulnerable leadership, service before self, and finding purpose. A must-read!"
—**Byron Bright,** President, KBR (a Fortune 500 Company)

"KC's experience comes out of these chapters. Whether in combat over Iraq or trying to help teams grow to become better, the perspective she has gained can help us all. This book displays those experiences and how they can be used. Her teachings in Character and Leadership to the Cadets of the Air Force Academy made a difference to future Air Force leaders. In this book, her teachings can make a difference for so many others."
—**Jay Silveria,** Lieutenant General, U.S. Air Force (Retired), 20th U.S.
    Air Force Academy Superintendent, Executive Director of Texas
    A&M University's Bush School of Government & Public Service,
    Washington DC

"Throughout her entire Air Force Career, Kim has been on the cutting edge of all the aspects of serving in our modern Air Force and leading people during challenging times both in peace and war. Her many leadership experiences as a fighter pilot, staff officer, and Commander, and her ability to balance both her personal and professional life in very stressful situations, have taught her how to expertly lead people and organizations. Her book, *Flying in the Face of Fear* is a must-read for anyone who wants to learn the many aspects of leadership both in today's military and in the complex world of business. Her real-life leadership experiences, which have made a positive difference in so many people's lives all over the world, have been written down in this book in an easy-to-understand format and will help the reader to become a better person and definitely a better leader for the 21st Century."
—**Stephen Lorenz,** General, U.S. Air Force (Retired), Former
    Commander, Air Education and Training Command

"*Flying in the Face of Fear* chronicles the remarkable life of USAF Colonel (retired) Kim Campbell—one of the few decorated female fighter pilots in US history—and shares important leadership lessons from which all of us can benefit. Through stories of both success and failure—at the Air Force Academy, in Afghanistan, Iraq and beyond—Kim offers a compelling formula for being successful by pushing through fear and leading through uncertainty."
—**Deborah Lee James,** 23rd Secretary of the Air Force

"*Flying in the Face of Fear: A Fighter Pilot's Lessons on Leading with Courage* by retired Air Force Colonel Kim 'KC' Campbell is a must-read for all leaders in today's challenging and divisive world. It is also an inspirational guide for future leaders within all sectors of society.

It is based upon leadership practices proven to be effective in all professions but told from the perspective of a woman combat fighter pilot who rose to become commander of a large Air Force unit, a senior Pentagon policy advisor, and an Air Force Academy professor and leader. Yet despite this prestigious combat, operational, policy, and academic record, she led a well-balanced personal and professional life. She often demonstrated the importance that her children played in her life to those who worked within her command.

The book is full of tips regarding how to become a highly effective leader, even when leading organizations in crisis or facing significant challenges. Her basic message is that all human beings encounter fear when facing difficult choices. The key is how to summon sufficient courage to overcome fear and make difficult choices. This ability is what makes a great leader in any sector. This book provides numerous examples of these choices.

Many additional aspects of this basic leadership principle are highlighted in the book. They range from perseverance to humility, respect, accountability, organization, and planning. The greatest leadership attributes remain courage, integrity, and balance.

I had the privilege of knowing Kim Campbell from the day she processed into the USAF Academy as a last-minute appointee; three years later she served as the top-ranked Cadet Wing Commander and graduated as a Marshall Scholar. I closely followed her progression throughout her Air Force career. She is widely respected as a highly decorated combat pilot, an inspirational senior commander, and a unique policy advisor. Read her book to discover the fundamentals of great leadership!"

—**Joseph G. Burke,** Colonel, U.S. Air Force (Retired), Ph.D.,
Tenured Professor, College President Emeritus, Senior Fellow,
Association of Governing Boards (AGB)

FLYING IN THE FACE OF FEAR

KIM "KC" CAMPBELL

COLONEL, U.S. AIR FORCE (RETIRED)

FLYING IN THE FACE OF FEAR

A **FIGHTER PILOT'S LESSONS** ON **LEADING WITH COURAGE**

WILEY

Published by John Wiley & Sons, Inc., Hoboken, New Jersey.
Published simultaneously in Canada.

For general information on our other products and services or for technical support, please contact our Customer Care Department within the United States at (800) 762-2974, outside the United States at (317) 572-3993 or fax (317) 572-4002.

Wiley also publishes its books in a variety of electronic formats. Some content that appears in print may not be available in electronic formats. For more information about Wiley products, visit our web site at www.wiley.com.

Library of Congress Cataloging-in-Publication Data Is Available:

ISBN 9781394298877 (Paperback)
ISBN 9781394152360 (ePub)
ISBN 9781394152377 (ePDF)

Cover Design: Wiley
Cover Images: A-10 Thunderbolt II by Master Sergeant Cecilio Ricardo |
© CPC Collection/Alamy Stock Photo, Pilot Photo Courtesy of the Author
Author Photo: Courtesy of the Author

SKY10093699_121224

For my boys, Colin and Brodie, who continue to teach me lessons about courage every day.

CONTENTS

Prologue: Seizing the Moment   *xv*

Chapter 1   Headwinds and Tailwinds   1

Chapter 2   Creating a Wingman Culture   17

Chapter 3   Fighter Pilot Mindset   35

Chapter 4   Prepare, Practice, Plan for Contingencies   51

Chapter 5   Wiggle Your Fingers and Toes   67

Chapter 6   Empower Your Wingmen   83

Chapter 7   The Fighter Pilot Debrief   105

Chapter 8   Aviate, Navigate, Communicate   119

Chapter 9   Recognize, Confirm, Recover   129

Chapter 10   Command and Connection   139

Chapter 11   Create Your Own Flight Plan   151

Chapter 12   Commander's Intent   173

Epilogue: Call to Action   183

Acknowledgments   197

Notes   199

About the Author   203

Index   205

PROLOGUE: SEIZING THE MOMENT

"I learned that courage was not the absence of fear, but the triumph over it. The brave man is not he who does not feel afraid, but he who conquers that fear."

—Nelson Mandela

Figure P.1 Operation Iraqi Freedom, 2003.
Photo credit: Alan Lessig, *Air Force Times*.

OVER BAGHDAD, IRAQ, 0741AM, 7 APRIL 2003

"My guys are taking fire in the northern part of town. Grid is Mike Bravo 396 990. Rocket propelled grenade teams are working on the east side of the Tigris River putting RPGs into my guys." I hear the frantic crackle over the radio in my cockpit.

Our role as A-10 pilots, our single reason for being is to support our troops on the ground. The moment an A-10 pilot hears the phrase "troops in contact," the only place we want to be is in the fight, overhead the troops on the ground. This day is no different, except low cloud cover over Baghdad means my flight lead and I are circling our A-10s high above the clouds and blind to the battle raging below. We know every second is an eternity for those fighting on the ground. We have to get a sense of the situation as quickly as possible, come up with our plan of action, and engage the enemy.

Our troops are on the west side of the Tigris River and small units of the Iraqi Republican Guard are on the east side of the river. The enemy is hiding under the North Baghdad Bridge and firing RPGs into our forces. Through static and intermittent machine gunfire, the ground controller explains the situation over the radio:

"We're hunkered down awaiting resupply, but our position has been compromised. Enemy troops are hiding underneath the overpass, coming out to shoot at our guys, and then returning to the overpass."

The clouds are both an obstacle and opportunity; while we can't see the target area, the enemy isn't aware of our presence. We stay above the clouds until the very last second, hoping to surprise the enemy. My flight lead goes first, disappearing through the clouds to get below the weather. Now it's my turn. I find a hole in the clouds and dive through. As soon as I get below the weather, I can see the firefight playing out below me. Muzzle flashes of carbines are interspersed with a steady stream of bright tracer rounds from heavy machine guns, creating a series of luminous arcs across the river. There is smoke in the air, and we are directly over the firefight, ready to attack. I focus on the firefight and look for our target. I set up to shoot my 30mm Gatling gun, when suddenly, I see puffs of gray and white smoke next to my cockpit. I realize the enemy isn't just shooting at our troops on the ground, they are shooting at us, too. But we have a mission to carry out so we continue with our attack.

"Yard 05, in from the north," my flight lead calls over the radio. He rolls his airplane toward the ground, aligning his gun to point right underneath the bridge where the enemy is hiding.

I am about one mile in trail, ready to follow up with his attack, when the ground controller shouts over the radio, "Yard 05, not effective, need you to come in from south to north."

I quickly abort my target run so we can maneuver our formation to set up for south-to-north target attacks. The south-to-north approach means we can hit the enemy hiding underneath the bridge, but it also makes us predictable because we can only ingress and egress from one direction. We decide we will only do two passes, then reassess the situation. It's my turn. I set up for my last rocket pass, check my altitude and distance from the target, and confirm my switches are set correctly. I roll the aircraft and point my nose at the ground. I am precisely where I want to be.

"Two's in from the south," I declare over the radio.

"Cleared hot, Two," comes the quick reply.

I fine-tune my aim point and press the weapons release button, rippling seven rockets down on the enemy. I immediately pull off target to get away from the ground and regain my altitude.

BOOM . . . I feel a large explosion at the back of my airplane and watch a bright red-orange fireball envelope my aircraft. My heart races, and my adrenaline pumps. Breathing rapidly against the pressure of my oxygen mask, my mouth becomes dry with the increase in oxygen flow. I quickly key the mic, "Two got hit. Two got hit."

The jet rolls over to the left and points directly down at Baghdad. In those few seconds looking outside of the cockpit, I can see the Tigris River getting closer, almost serene against the drab desert surrounding both sides of the winding water. As my jet plummets completely out of control, I instinctively pull back on the control stick. But nothing—absolutely nothing—happens. Baghdad is getting closer, and I know I might have to eject. But the last thing I want to do is eject out of my airplane and into the hands of the enemy. I have visions of descending quietly down in a parachute into the hands of an enraged enemy whose comrades we had just killed. It isn't a good option.

My flight lead provides immediate guidance, "Copy, bring it back west, try and come west."

I vaguely hear his response as I quickly try to analyze the situation:

Master caution light.
Hydraulic lights.
Hydraulic gauges are at zero. The system has no pressure. It's empty.

I am plunging to the ground completely out of control in a 45,000-pound airplane filled to the brim with fuel and explosives. I'm in a left-hand turn, and my left wing is slicing through the sky. There is no sound now except for the static on my radio. I look down at my yellow-and -black striped ejection handles. There is a bright green grassy area on the east side of the river, just north of the bridge. Can I manage to land my parachute there and attempt to evade capture? No, not yet. I'm not ready to take the risk of falling into enemy hands. I don't think that would be a pleasant experience based on the knowledge we have about what the Iraqi Republican Guard has done to previous prisoners. My flight lead's voice breaks through my troublesome thoughts, "Say your position. Got you. Turn west. Chaff, Flare. Chaff, Flare. Turn it west."

I immediately push down on the chaff and flare buttons, dispensing metallic clouds of chaff and bright burning flares from my aircraft in hopes of decoying additional enemy missiles. I can hear my flight lead's directions and I know I need to get my airplane over the west side of the river. If I have to eject, I can ideally float down over friendly forces and not be immediately captured by the enemy. Unfortunately, my airplane won't maneuver. It won't climb, it won't turn, it's just plummeting. My time is running out.

I need to make every second count. If I make the wrong decision, then I will lose time, and I could die trying. I was not giving up. I set aside my fear and focus on taking action. I flip the switch on the left side of my cockpit labeled MANUAL REVERSION.

In an instant, the airplane transitions from hydraulics to a manual flight control mode, now flying on old-school cranks and cables. I pull back on the stick again, and this time, the airplane starts to climb. I am flooded with relief. The green waters of the Tigris River and the brown sandy banks fade away as I finally see white clouds and hints of blue sky appear out my windscreen. The North Baghdad Bridge disappears behind me as I start a gradual left turn to evade the target area and the enemy. It has been less than 20 seconds since my airplane was hit, but to me, it feels like an eternity.

My flight lead is worried and calmly asks, "How are you doing?"

My voice is shaky, but I reply, "I'm alright. I'm in manual reversion, it's flying fine. I'm going west."

As I gain altitude, I can finally see the sun shining above the clouds. I just want to get above the weather and away from Baghdad. My breathing slowly returns to normal as I make my way above the clouds. For the first time, I think I might make it out of here alive. My flight lead radios to our ground controller, "Advance, we're out of here. My number-two man is hit."

"Copy that . . . good luck," the ground controller hesitantly radios back, not quite sure what to say.

Despite my initial sense of relief, the hard part is yet to come. I know I have to decide whether to land the jet or get to friendly territory and eject. My flight lead confirms the reality of the situation, "You need to start thinking if you want to try and land it or jump out. That is your decision and your decision only."

The decision feels like it could be the difference between life and death, and it weighs heavily on me. A lifetime of training has prepared me for this moment, but there is no guarantee I will make it out alive. I can't allow myself to think about the fear that is creeping in. Those feelings and emotions will have to wait until I am safely on the ground.

IN RETROSPECT

The truth is, surviving that combat mission over Baghdad was one of the most terrifying experiences of my life. But admit I was scared? I was supposed to be a tough, fearless fighter pilot. I couldn't admit it then—it's taken me years to admit it, understand it, and realize how recognizing and acknowledging fear can help me act with courage.

I've been scared many times in my life, just like we all have. It can be hard to admit when we're scared, stressed, or worried about something. And I'm not just talking about the fear associated with life-or-death situations or flying a fighter jet in combat. Fear is fear. It's about fear of failure, fear of not meeting expectations, fear of change, fear of the unknown. It can all be daunting and stressful, but what matters is what we do when we are scared. It's about our actions in the face of fear. It's about having the courage to respond even *when* we're scared.

The lessons learned from that mission set the stage for the rest of my life . . . for flying future missions in combat, for raising two young kids while my husband deployed, and for leading more than 1,000 military and civilian personnel as a group commander. In each of these situations, there were times when I felt fear. It's not uncommon to feel stressed, worried, or even scared about the challenges we're facing. And sometimes when we feel that way, instead of taking action, the fear of judgment and failure can paralyze us. So, we do nothing. We resist change. We avoid hard conversations. We fail to hold each other accountable. But how can we improve if we don't learn from our failures and mistakes? How can we excel in a competitive environment if we don't push ourselves outside our comfort zone? Fear can prevent us from achieving success, or it can lead us to a greater path of growth and change if we harness it effectively. So as hard as it may be, we need to have the courage to persevere through challenges, do the hard things, and take action even in the face of fear. When we take action in critical moments, when we persevere despite the difficulty, then we are positioned to create a culture of courage and an environment of trust that builds deeper relationships, inspires loyalty, and enables our team to perform at their best.

If leaders are going to be successful in complex, rapidly changing environments, then we need to lead with courage. In a study conducted by best-selling author and researcher, Brené Brown, for her book *Dare to Lead*, 150 global leaders were asked about the future of leadership and what skills were needed for a leader to be successful. One clear theme across all interviews was that we need braver leaders and more courageous cultures.[1] We can make a significant impact on our team when we have the courage to face adversity, take action in difficult situations, and lead our team through challenges. We need courageous leaders. It takes courage to hold ourselves and others accountable, to have difficult conversations, and to make decisions when we don't have perfect information. It also takes courage to get out and connect with our team and to reveal the human side of leadership. When we act with courage, then our team is likely to do the same. And when we lead with courage, then we create an environment in which our team can excel.

Flying in the Face of Fear shares my leadership journey as a combat-proven fighter pilot and senior military leader. Fighter pilot culture is unique. We spend our lives working in a high-stakes environment, where we have to make split-second decisions to survive, and where training missions can be just as dangerous as actual combat.

In a fighter squadron, we learn quickly that the strength of the team is determined by the individuals who make up the team. From the newest wingman to the most experienced instructor, we come to know how each of us plays a distinctive role on the team and how our contributions are critical for our shared success. We clearly understand our roles and responsibilities and how we fit into the bigger picture. We also realize the importance of holding each other accountable and creating a culture of continuous improvement.

Fighter pilots embrace vulnerability to learn through our successes as well as our failures, some of the most vital lessons coming from friends and teammates we've lost in aircraft mishaps along the way. Because of our high-risk environment, we have developed distinctive leadership techniques and principles that are tested under extreme stress, both in training and combat. These techniques and principles enable us to inspire and empower high-performing teams to succeed.

The lessons I share stem from my successes and failures during my military career, and they are also relevant for leaders outside the military environment. While there is no singular recipe for leadership success, these proven principles have worked for me in training and combat with teams of all sizes. They have also worked for the leaders I've trained and mentored throughout my 24 years of service and beyond. This book is my story of facing fears and leading with courage as a fighter pilot, military leader, mom, and wife. I hope to help leaders deal with challenging and stressful situations, face their fears, and persevere in the face of adversity. *Flying in the Face of Fear* is a collection of lessons and stories that will serve as a resource for any leader who is willing to make an impact and a difference with the teams they lead.

Chapter 1

HEADWINDS AND TAILWINDS

"When everything seems to be going against you, remember that the airplane takes off against the wind, not with it."
—Henry Ford

Figure 1.1 I experienced my first flight in a Cessna as a Civil Air Patrol cadet at San Jose International Airport. I was hooked!

LEARNING TO FLY

"It's all yours. You have control." Control. The word echoed in my mind on repeat. I feel the sweat beads forming on my forehead. My hands are clammy, and my entire body is shaking. My stomach is a trapeze artist doing flips in the air. This is it! I have control!

The clear blue sky stretches out before me, and for miles around there is not another airplane to be seen. I glance down only to find a miniature town adorning a distant and unknown land. It is my turn to maneuver the precious metal. I turn the control handle to the right and to my surprise, the airplane rolls to the right. I turn the handle to the left and the plane rolls left. I shiver with excitement as the airplane maneuvers at my command.

I did it! It is the greatest feeling to know that I have control of something that had the potential to take me anywhere I wanted to go. I am free and there is nothing more I could ask for. I soar into the sunset knowing that I have accomplished my dream. I had flown an airplane!

I put these words to paper when I was 16 years old after flying a small airplane for the first time. Fifteen flights later, I earned the opportunity to solo. I taxi down the taxiways at San Jose International Airport behind enormous passenger airlines in a little Cessna all by myself. The thrill of a solo takeoff is indescribable. There is no instructor to tell me what to do or to help me with my landings. It's all me. I'm excited and scared at the same time. I did a few touch-and-go landings — not the best landings I had ever done, but I learned early in my career that any landing you can walk away from is a good one.

After I land, my instructor, Carol Tevebaugh, cuts the back of my shirt to hang on the bulletin board at the flying club. Cutting the shirttail after a student completes their first solo flight is a tradition in the aviation community. Most early training aircraft had tandem seating (one in front of the other, with the student in front). Before headset technology, an instructor would commonly have to tug on the back of the student's shirt to get their attention. Cutting the shirttail off was a rite of passage, showing that the instructor now had confidence in the student's abilities and no longer required the same hands-on assistance. After flying solo, I became even more convinced that this flying thing was definitely for me. I was not a natural at flying, but I could work hard and be good at it. I loved the thrill of taking off and the challenge of trying to get better. Flying made me feel free.

ADJUSTING FOR WINDS

Wind is one of the main factors affecting an aircraft's flight. Headwinds blow directly in front of an aircraft, opposing forward motion. During flight, headwinds can slow us down, requiring more fuel to get where we need to go. However, to create lift on takeoff, an airplane will take off into the wind. The same concept applies to life and leadership. Headwinds are obstacles we need to overcome. When we face headwinds, we may experience fear and doubt about our ability to get where we want to go. We may even have to divert to refuel before getting back on the route to our destination. Overcoming headwinds is key to perseverance. And when we overcome headwinds in life, it will make us stronger and more resilient. Headwinds may slow us down, but they also give us lift.

A tailwind, on the other hand, is wind blowing in the direction of travel. Tailwinds can help us go faster and conserve fuel. In life, tailwinds occur when things are going our way. Although we prefer to operate in smooth tailwinds, we don't always have that option, so we must prepare to face the wind and adjust accordingly. We don't have control over the wind, but we do have control over our planning and preparation, as well as our response to the wind we encounter. Adjusting for headwinds and tailwinds became a principle for how I approached life's challenges. Learning to adjust expectations, actions, thoughts, and responses is key to navigating life effectively.

TAKING OFF

On January 28, 1986, my mom and I were sitting in our living room in San Jose, California, watching TV when the news came on. The world around me did not matter for 72 seconds as I watched the launch of the space shuttle *Challenger*. On the 73rd second, the *Challenger* turned into a horrifying ball of smoke and flames in an explosion that killed everyone aboard.

I cried. I had no idea why, but I cried as if I knew the astronauts personally. "Why would anyone risk their life like that?" I asked.

My mom, an oncology nurse, turned to me with tears in her eyes. "There are some things in life more important than yourself. Doing what you believe in sometimes means risking your life."

It took me some time to understand the gravity of my feelings. Why was I so emotionally connected to these astronauts I didn't even know? At age 10, I knew they died doing something they believed in, something important. But even 37 years later, I struggle to make sense of it all. The astronauts had a dream they chased. And even though they failed to reach the stars, they were committed to a vision that was big and important, not just for them, but for the rest of the world.

It was at that moment I realized I wanted to commit my life to something bigger, something more important than myself. I wanted to serve and believe so strongly in something that I would be willing to give my life in pursuit of it. As I watched that shuttle launch, something drew me toward the exhilaration of flight and the sense of freedom and fearlessness that goes with it. At that moment, my future began to take shape, and I knew what I wanted. I wrote it down on a gold star that would hang from my bedroom ceiling throughout middle school and high school . . . "Reach for the Stars!"

BEYOND DREAMS

I know now, of course, that setting a goal is the easy part. Only years of hard work can make it a reality. Then sometimes, it still does not turn out the way we plan. There are struggles and challenges along the way, ups and downs; it's a wild ride to try to get to those stars. However, the payoff can be worth it. That is why we dream. That is why we set goals of going to the stars.

One night, shortly after watching coverage of the *Challenger* accident, I asked my dad how I could become an astronaut. He glanced at me with a look of surprise. Before this sudden conversation, my future career interests had included being an actor or a pediatrician. After a moment of hesitation, he told me that many of the astronauts were pilots in the Air Force, and many of those pilots had gone to the Air Force Academy.

I didn't know anything about the Academy, so I bombarded Dad with questions. "What is it like? What does it take to get there? What do I need to do to get accepted?" I had an endless list. After hearing all his answers, I decided right then, attending the Air Force Academy was my goal. I would go there and become a fighter pilot.

Even though my dad maintained his stoic attorney's face during this conversation, he recounted years later what he was thinking. "I experienced mixed emotions. I was pleased she would aspire to do it, but all too aware of what she would go through."

My dad graduated from the Air Force Academy with the Class of 1970. There were no women admitted to the Academy at that time, so it was tough for him to think about his little girl suffering through the punishing physical and mental training everyone endured at the Academy. On June 28, 1976, 156 women became the first female cadets to enter the Air Force Academy. The Class of 1980 was the first to graduate women, with 97 women graduating that year. In 1986, when I decided I wanted to go to the Air Force Academy, only about 10% of cadets were women.

It never occurred to me that my dream of being a fighter pilot could be limited based on my gender. After all, there were two women on the space shuttle *Challenger*, astronaut Judith Resnik and teacher Christa McAuliffe. I had no idea at the time that laws prevented women from being fighter pilots. In 1986, regulations excluded women from nearly one-half of all military positions throughout the armed forces. In the Air Force specifically, women could not fly in combat aircraft until the rules eventually changed in 1993. My parents never told me that. They could have told me that women could not be fighter pilots, that it would be a long, hard road to go against the rules and norms of the time. Instead, they just let me pursue my dream. They told me to work hard and go after what I wanted.

My dad also thought I might lose interest over time and come up with a new career path. According to my parents, I had been more of a social butterfly than a scholar or athlete before the *Challenger* accident. My only competitive activities up to this point had been beauty pageants. Studying and homework were burdens. When I continued to talk about the Academy, my dad decided to tell me the things I needed to do to prepare. He did not want to discourage me, but he knew I had to be prepared to survive life at the Academy. He still thought once I saw how hard it would be, I might lose interest.

I never lost interest. To me, all the challenges and difficulties would be worth it if I could graduate from the Academy and become a fighter pilot. I was confident I could overcome the hurdles by arriving mentally and physically prepared. My fixation on going to the Academy drove my behavior at school and at home. To my parents' great relief, I became completely self-motivated with my schoolwork. They never had to tell me to do my homework. According to my parents, it was as if I flipped a switch. I stayed loyal to my goal of going to the Air Force Academy, and after a few years of proving myself at school, my dad concluded I was seriously committed, and this was not just a fleeting idea. However, he wasn't sure if I was tough enough to handle the rigorous training.

GOOD ENOUGH FOR A GIRL

My first, but certainly not my last, experience of being in a male-dominated environment began on my first day of woodshop class in middle school. I had decided to take woodshop as one of my electives. I had always enjoyed making things so I thought this would be a fun class to take. Most of the other students in the class were boys and the teacher was an older man who had taught at the school for years. One of the projects we had to make was a wooden pencil case. I finished the primary design and was getting ready to stain the wood but decided I would check with my teacher first.

"What do you think?" I asked.

He looked at the pencil case, smiled at me, and responded, "It's good enough for a girl."

I was confused. *Good enough for a girl?! What does that even mean?* I could feel my blood pressure rise and my face turn red. *How could he say that to me?* I wanted to quit and walk out of his classroom. I also knew that would not help my grade. I took my pencil case and went back to my workstation feeling defeated, but determined to do better and prove him wrong.

I decided to use my teacher's comments as motivation. To this day, I don't know what his true intent was in saying that to me, but I never wanted to be just "good enough" at anything. I wanted to be good at what I did. Period. Respected for what I did. Whether he intended to or not, he lit a fire in me. I vowed never to be just "good enough." I was going to excel.

FACING THE HEADWINDS

I poured everything I had into getting selected for the Air Force Academy, but I also experienced an occasional sense of doubt. *Was I good enough? Was there anything else I could do to improve?* That small sense of doubt became part of my motivation to keep working hard to improve.

I got good grades in school and was a member of the National Honor Society. My big challenge was the SAT. It turns out my SAT scores were not that great, and they were below average for competitive candidates at the Air Force Academy. I took the SAT five separate times, in addition to an SAT class to help prepare, and I still ended up with the same score every time. It was extremely frustrating. I was still hopeful that my grades and extracurricular activities, like being senior class president, would help make up for my below-average SAT performance.

The key, according to the Air Force Academy Admissions Office, was to be well rounded, to be good at every aspect of Academy life. On the physical fitness side, I was captain of the cheerleading squad and played sports, lettering in soccer, track, and cross-country. Although I felt my high school accomplishments were notable, the more I looked at statistics about Air Force Academy cadets, the more angst it generated because the stats made me feel average.

According to statistics released by the Air Force Academy about the class of 1997: 72% were members of the National Honors Society, 85% lettered in athletics, 90% were in the top 20% of their high school class, and 22% were class presidents or vice presidents. Although stats like these made me feel average, they also helped increase my motivation to perform and work hard to excel.

The Air Force Academy application process was intensive. One of the key components to the application was an interview and recommendation from my admissions liaison officer, Lieutenant Colonel Dana Arbaugh. I didn't know it at the time, but on my recommendation form to attend the Academy, he made the following recommendation and prediction:

> *Kim Reed is a future* Cadet Wing Commander. *She is the most motivated, capable, and personable candidate I have encountered in my 12 years as a liaison officer. She first contacted me at the beginning of her freshman year to express her strong desire for the Academy and an Air Force career. She has contacted me on a regular basis since then, both for advice and to keep me informed of her superb progress. With her strong academic and leadership abilities, and charismatic personality, I predict that as an Air Force Academy Cadet, Kim will be on the Superintendent's list all four years.*

I would have a lot to live up to as a cadet at the Air Force Academy. But first, I needed to get through the application process successfully. The Air Force Academy's acceptance rate is roughly 11%. Out of approximately 10,000 applications, only 1,164 cadets would be admitted to the Class of 1997. It wasn't going to be easy, but it was a goal I wasn't willing to give up on.

POWER WOMEN

Throughout high school, I thankfully had coaches, teachers, and mentors who encouraged and supported me along the way. Nancy Kennett, my English teacher and speech and debate coach, really pushed us to go after what we wanted. She called us "power women" because she believed in us and wanted us to do what we were capable of without letting politics or policy get in the way. She encouraged us to be change-makers in society. One of my speeches for her class centered on women in combat. Here were a few of my thoughts at the time:

> *Women join the armed forces for much the same reason men have—excitement, travel, patriotism, and a chance for skills they could not get elsewhere. . . Women want to serve their country just as men do.*

We have made some progress in women's rights, but until women are allowed to carry out the same missions as men, our rights will not be equal.

I was starting to realize and understand the career path I planned had limits for women. It would be easy to get discouraged based on the rules and policies at the time, but thankfully, I had parents, mentors, and teachers who encouraged me to go after what I wanted. Mrs. Kennett's yearbook post to me said, "To a total Power Woman! I'm counting on you to go out and change the world—it needs changing and it needs Kim Reed." Quite a difference from my middle school experience, but those words also encouraged me to pursue my goals and work hard at what I wanted.

PROVING IT

Military members are known for their mental and physical toughness. My dad knew this firsthand based on his own experience, which was why he wondered if I was tough enough to go to the Academy. Military training is full of both mental and physical challenges. Studies have shown that most often, the mind quits before the body does. During military training, instructors push you to your limits to see how you will respond. Will you give in and quit? The question becomes, how do we judge mental and physical toughness for men and women desiring to attend military academies? Is there an indicator that can prove or disprove success?

It turns out that a high school cross-country race would offer my first big test of perseverance as well as mental and physical toughness. We ran our cross-country races at Alum Rock Park in San Jose. We would start in the parking lot as a massive group and then make our way to the dirt trails in the hills for the two-mile race. For those of us who thrive on competition, the start to a cross-country race was always exciting since everyone crammed in together, trying to vie for a spot out front. As the starting gun sounded, I sprinted to make my way through the maze of runners. Somewhere in the middle of the pack, another runner stepped on the back of my shoe, and it came off. I had a split-second of hesitation . . . do I stop and try to find my shoe in the chaos and then take the time to put it back on, or do I keep running? Stopping would take too much time. I kept running. The dust finally cleared with all the runners making their way into the hills. The coaches were anxiously awaiting our return when they realized there was a running shoe left behind. My coach, Tracie Frandsen, looked at it, and said, "That has to be Kim's shoe. Only Kim Reed would do something like that."

I would run the entire two-mile race without a shoe. I did not win the race, but I still made a suitable time. I could hear the comments as I came close to the finish line, "She doesn't have a shoe on! Who runs without a shoe?" My coach smiled at me as I crossed the finish line and said, "I knew it was you!"

My mom and brother were at the race that day to cheer me on, but they didn't notice I was running without a shoe until after I crossed the finish line. They came over to congratulate me, found me lying in the grass with a bloody blistered foot, and then realized what I had done. I was crying and laughing at the same time. I was in pain, but I was laughing at the crazy idea I had to keep going and finish the race without a shoe. My mom quickly went into nurse mode. She laughed and asked what I was thinking. Through tears, I replied, "I didn't want to be held back. I didn't want to lose."

Looking back, my mom said she thought I was a little crazy, but she was proud of me, too, for not quitting, for not giving up. That decision earned me a trip to the hospital, but it also earned me credibility as a tough and determined athlete.

Most important, that decision had another significant impact on my future. My mom called my dad at work right after the race to tell him what had happened. He later told me his first thought was, "I guess she is tough enough to go to the Academy."

My dad decided right then that he would do everything possible to help me prepare. That night as we sat at the dinner table, he told me if I planned to go to the Academy, then I needed to be prepared. It was as if I earned my way into his world of experience as a cadet. Who knew that a split-second decision about running without a shoe would have such a significant impact?

As we ate dinner that night, we came up with a plan to ensure I would be ready to take the Candidate Fitness Test. The test included push-ups, pull-ups, sit-ups, as well as a shuttle run, so I knew I had to prepare physically. I was playing soccer and running cross-country in high school, but I did not have a lot of upper body strength. We installed a pull-up bar in my bathroom so each time I went in and out of the bathroom I would do as many pull-ups as possible. To start with, I could not do a single pull-up.

Figure 1.2   Running the high school cross-country league finals without a shoe. My decision to keep going after losing a shoe earned respect from my teammates and fellow competitors.

I could only do the flexed arm hang, but I worked my way up to one, then two, and eventually to the women's Physical Fitness Test maximum of eight pull-ups. We also started running the hills around my house in combat boots so I could make sure they were broken in and blisters would not slow me down. I'm sure the neighbors thought we were crazy, but it helped me prepare. Those experiences also created a bond with my dad that has remained over the years. Dad was my role model and hero, and I looked up to him and trusted his advice. I still do.

DECISION TIME

On April 23, 1993, I pulled into our driveway in my red Honda Prelude, jumped out and raced over to the mailbox, a daily tradition as I waited in anticipation for an acceptance letter from the Air Force Academy. I opened the mailbox and shuffled through the letters, looking for the prestigious Academy stationery. This day, the bright blue letters caught my eye, and I ripped open the envelope with excitement. It was finally here.

Dear Kim,

I regret to inform you that you will not be offered an appointment to the Air Force Academy this year. Your excellent record qualifies you for admission, but we are limited in size by public law and cannot appoint everyone who is qualified. . . . With almost 10,000 outstanding young people competing to be among the approximately 1,200 admitted, the competition for appointment was extremely keen this year. . . . Kim, I appreciate your interest in attending the Air Force Academy and wish you the very best in all of your future endeavors.

What?! Shock. Devastation. I didn't know what to do. I stood there on the side of the street near the open mailbox, letter in hand, in complete disbelief. *What now?*

This was all I had ever wanted. I poured my heart and soul into being accepted, and the Academy said no. I wasn't good enough. I had done everything I could. I had worked so hard and focused on nothing else. And the Academy said it was not enough. I called my parents at work to tell them the news. They were crushed. They knew how much I wanted this. I had applied and been accepted to other schools (only because my parents made me apply to have a backup plan), but I never really considered going anywhere else. The Academy was the only school I wanted to attend.

I hesitantly called Colonel Arbaugh to tell him the news as well. He told me later he was not particularly surprised because his indications were that I might be rejected based on my SAT scores. He told me not to give up. He suggested I write to the Academy and let them know I was still interested and to convince them I was not giving up. I thought it was a little crazy and likely not going to work, but I wanted this so badly I was willing to try anything. That was a defining moment for me. I had faced a crushing blow and I could respond in one of two ways: give up and find something new or keep trying and working to achieve my goal. I decided I was not going to give up.

I sent letters to the Academy every week telling them how much I wanted to attend and what I had done to improve my scores. I would tell them about an A on a test or that I could do five more pushups. I eventually took the ACT and significantly improved my scores, so I ensured the Academy had that information as well. I wanted the admissions office to know I was immediately available for a late offer of appointment. If someone decided the Academy was not for them, then I was ready and willing to go. I was so motivated to attend the Academy that I had plans to show up to the Academy on in-processing day to be available if someone else didn't show up or was too scared to get off the bus.

As the weeks went on, I continued my letter-writing campaign but also knew my chances were diminishing with each week that passed. High school graduation was approaching, and I knew I needed a plan. I reluctantly decided to commit to a Reserve Officer Training Corps (ROTC) scholarship at the University of California, San Diego. It was a terrific opportunity, but my heart was not in it. The weeks passed and my heart sank. Maybe this wasn't going to work after all. I kept checking the mailbox, but my confidence was wavering. Then on Wednesday, June 2, 1993, another letter in the mailbox came . . .

> *Dear Kim*
>
> *Congratulations! On behalf of the Superintendent, it is my pleasure to announce your appointment to the United States Air Force Academy as a member of the Class of 1997. You will be joining a select group of our nation's finest young people as you take this challenging and rewarding step toward becoming a professional Air Force officer. . . . I compliment you on an excellent record of personal achievement and look forward to welcoming you to the Cadet Wing on July 1, 1993.*

Yes! I took the letter and raced back to school to share my excitement with all my friends and teachers who were always supportive of me and my goals. They were ecstatic! They had shared in my disappointment, and now they could share in my success.

BRING ME MEN

On the morning of July 1, 1993, I arrived at the base of the Bring Me Men ramp to begin my journey. The line "Bring Me Men" comes from the poem, *The Coming American*, by Sam Walter Foss. For 39 years, the most famous line from this poem adorned the base of a ramp where cadets form up and march down to the Parade Field.

Bring me men to match my mountains,
  Men to match their majesty.
  Men to climb beyond their summits,
  Searching for their destiny.
  These are men to build a nation,
  Join the mountains to the sky,
  Men of faith and inspiration,
  Bring me men, bring me men, bring me men!

That ramp was a bridge to our future life and all that it could be. I felt sick to my stomach and excited at the same time. I was nervous about what was to come, the fear of the unknown. It certainly would not be the first time in my career that I would face challenges, stress, and fear. Nevertheless, this would be my first Air Force test. It was finally time. All the training and preparation had finally paid off. I had worked so hard to get here. I just had to take a few more steps to commit. I stopped for a quick picture below the Bring Me Men ramp and then took my first steps across the line. My time at the Academy had officially begun.

LOOKING BACK

I often think back to my journey leading up to my arrival at the Air Force Academy. *What if I had quit when times got tough? What if I hadn't worked harder to improve?* I think about all the opportunities and experiences I would have missed. Although challenging and sometimes painful, these experiences made me realize how important it is to go hard after our goals and dreams. We need to be willing to put in the work to make them happen. If it's not going well, we need to take the initiative to try a different approach. We will hear the word *no* and face rejection endlessly. People are watching to see how we handle adversity. It's okay to feel disappointed or angry in the moment (I certainly did), but then we need to get back in the game. Rejection can be painful, but it can also motivate us to do better, to be open to opportunities for change, and to grow stronger. Keep after it, work hard, and have a good attitude.

Dr. Angela Duckworth, professor of psychology and best-selling author of the book, *Grit: The Power of Passion and Perseverance,* describes this concept as grit. "Grit is passion and perseverance for long-term goals . . . grit is about having what some researchers call an 'ultimate concern'—a goal you care about so much that it organizes and gives meaning to almost everything you do. And grit is holding steadfast to that goal. Even when you fall down. Even when you screw up. Even when progress toward that goal is halting or slow."[1]

CONSIDERATIONS FOR LEADERS

Leaders must demonstrate grit, fortitude, and perseverance. When things don't go as planned, when times are tough, we must show up with our words and actions, making it clear we will face adversity and overcome challenges. We will get back up again when we get knocked down. Learn from past mistakes and do it better the next time. Don't quit. Keep pressing on. We need to be able to show our team that we have grit, that we won't let tough times stop us. As Duckworth explains, "If you're a leader, and you want the people in your organization to be grittier, create a gritty culture."[2] Leaders need to understand how we can make an impact and a difference when our teammates are faced with challenges. *How do we best respond? What difference will we make?* When our team faces adversity, we can make a positive impact by taking these actions:

- Investing in and caring about our people
- Encouraging our teammates to get back up, to keep pressing forward when they fall
- Reminding our teammates (and ourselves) that failure can be a painful experience, but in the long run, it will make us stronger and more resilient

Headwinds may slow us down, but they also give us lift. **If you want to lead with courage, then turn into the wind. Have confidence that you can tackle the challenges that come your way.**

Chapter 2

CREATING
A WINGMAN CULTURE

"Alone we can do so little; together we can do so much."
—Helen Keller

Figure 2.1 Leading the 4,000-member Cadet Wing during noon meal formation at the United States Air Force Academy.

I joined the Air Force to commit my life to something bigger, something more important than myself. I wanted to serve. I quickly learned through my time at the Air Force Academy that it was never about me; it was about the team. The Air Force Academy introduced us to the importance of the wingman concept, a promise and commitment between airmen to take care of themselves and those around them. It was all about "fostering a culture of Airmen taking care of Airmen."[1] We were taught to never leave a wingman behind; we were always there to provide mutual support.

So how do we make good wingmen? How do we create a wingman culture where each person is part of something bigger and more important than themselves? At the Air Force Academy I learned to be part of a team, understanding that the strength of the team was based on the individuals who made up the team. We had to work together and support each other if we were going to succeed.

MAKING OF A CADET

"Get your chins in! Shoulders up, back, and down!"

It is Thursday, July 1, 1993, when 1,164 young men and women from all walks of life arrive at the base of the Bring Me Men ramp ready for basic training on this warm and sunny Colorado day.

The Class of 1997 includes basic cadets from every state in the nation. There are eight international students from Colombia, Morocco, Nigeria, Pakistan, Poland, Sri Lanka, Thailand, and Turkey. Training with foreign military cadets exposes us to foreign military cultures and diverse ways of thinking. It is an early lesson in working together to increase cooperation and partnership. The class also includes 31 sons and 14 daughters of Service Academy graduates from the Air Force Academy, West Point, Annapolis, and the Coast Guard Academy.

Screaming upperclassmen (also known as *cadre*) greet us while trying to get us into the rigid position of attention. Once we attain some semblance of military formation, we can begin the march up the Bring Me Men ramp. The march up the ramp marks our entrance into the Air Force Academy. On graduation day, if we make it, we then march down the ramp, departing the Air Force Academy on our way to becoming Air Force officers.

As we march single file carrying only our duffel bags, I want to scream with excitement and simultaneously hide in fear. More than anything, I just want to blend in with the basic cadets in front of and behind me. Basic Cadet Training (BCT), better known as Beast, is about to begin.

At the top of the ramp, the BCT cadre again greet us and give us a checklist to carry as we collect the gear we would need during BCT. I am supposed to keep my eyes straightforward looking at the head of the basic cadet in front of me, but I'm anxious to get a glimpse of the cadet area where I would spend the next four years. The main buildings in the cadet area surround an open space known as the terrazzo. The name comes from the walkway's terrazzo tiles that are set among a checkerboard of marble strips. During our first year, we could only run on the marble strips to get to and from locations in the cadet area, stopping only to greet upper-class cadets along the way: "Good afternoon, Sir! Huge Wild Weasels." (The name of my soon-to-be cadet squadron, a tribute to the pilots who flew enemy air defense suppression missions during Vietnam).

There is a hierarchy at the Academy, and it quickly becomes clear that we are at the bottom.

To the outsider, some of these traditions may seem like silly nonsense. However, each nickname, each squadron logo, has roots from our past. Joining the military and attending the Air Force Academy meant we would become part of the Long Blue Line. The Long Blue Line refers to all the Academy graduates who came before us—those who made history, those who gave back to the next generation, and those who died serving their country.

I can see the iconic cadet chapel in the distance, aircraft on display, and the air gardens with 700 feet of lighted pools. It is a stunning campus, but you don't notice the beauty during basic cadet training. Its beauty, symbolism, and audacity are seen and felt only in retrospect.

On our first day, we walk through warehouses and brightly lit hallways in Fairchild Hall. We are processed through dozens of stations where we receive brown plastic hangers, athletic socks, boot socks, t-shirts, as well as underwear and pajamas that look like something your grandparents might wear. Everything from haircuts to immunizations to dental examinations are doled out in assembly-line fashion. It is a long and exhausting day. We learn quickly that we can only talk in the form of the Seven Basic Responses:

1. *Yes Sir/Ma'am!*
2. *No Sir/Ma'am!*
3. *No excuse, Sir/Ma'am!*
4. *Sir/Ma'am, may I make a statement?*
5. *Sir/Ma'am, may I ask a question?*
6. *Sir/Ma'am, I do not understand.*
7. *Sir/Ma'am, I do not know.*

This is our new way of life, and there are distinct ways of doing things. We are no longer team captains or valedictorians. We are simply basic cadets. Everything we did to get to this point doesn't matter anymore. By design, the Academy brings people in from all walks of life, breaks down any perceived hierarchies, then teaches us the military hierarchy. We would learn a new set of values required for all Air Force Academy cadets: integrity, service, and excellence. These values would stay with us for the rest of our military careers.

The first day was overwhelming. There was so much to take in and mounting apprehension about what would come next. We no longer had control of our lives. Cadre told us what to do and when to do it. We had come to the Academy at the top of our class, in charge of our future, and now the cadre broke us down, mentally and physically, to teach us how to face uncertainty, to be resilient, and to work together as a team in order to survive.

As we ended our first day, the cadre gave us Air Force Academy stationery to write a letter home about the first day of BCT.

> *Dear Mom & Dad,*
>
> *I'm finally here. We did a lot of walking and a lot of waiting today. We went through forty-two different stations for in-processing. I can't believe that I'm actually here. Well, today wasn't so bad, but I know as soon we take the oath (tomorrow) it's going to get a lot worse. I can do it though!*

The next day, we marched out on the terrazzo to face the class wall, which held every class crest of those who had come before us. We raised our right hands to take the oath of office:

> *I, Kim Nichole Reed, do solemnly swear that I will support and defend the Constitution of the United States against all enemies, foreign and domestic; that I will bear true faith and allegiance to the same; that I take this obligation freely, without any mental reservation or purpose of evasion; and that I will well and faithfully discharge the duties of the office upon which I am about to enter. So help me God.*

This would be the first time, but certainly not the last, that I would swear to support and defend the Constitution of the United States. The oath signifies a serious commitment and desire to serve.

As I took the oath for the first time, I felt overwhelmed with emotion. I had worked so hard to get here. As I swore to support and defend the Constitution of the United States, I felt an overwhelming sense of pride. This was what I was meant to do. I was meant to be here. All the difficulties I had faced trying to get into the Academy didn't matter anymore. I was here. Now, I just had to survive BCT.

BCT at the Air Force Academy is broken up into two phases. In the first two weeks, the cadre taught us the basics of military customs and courtesies, how to wear the uniform, and how to march. We would wake up early every morning to banging on the doors, shouts from upperclassmen, as well as music blaring in the hallways. "Welcome to the Jungle" by Guns N' Roses was a crowd favorite. During the day, we endured room inspections, physical training, and classes about the Cadet Honor Code. Meals were opportunities to question us about knowledge; eating was something to be done only in the last few minutes of the meal, cramming in every calorie we could before enduring more physical exercise.

With each experience, we learned the importance of attention to detail, discipline, time management, and working together as a team. These qualities helped us survive at the Academy and were early lessons that stayed with us throughout our military career. One of the things we had to memorize was the purpose of the fourth-class system at the Academy:

> *The purpose of the fourth-class system at the United States Air Force Academy is to lay the foundation early in the cadet's career for the development of these qualities of character and discipline which will be expected of an officer. These qualities must be so deeply instilled in the individual's personality that no stress or strain will erase them.*

We learned to perform under stress and to endure despite difficulties. BCT officially began our transition from civilian to military life. Because of my time in Civil Air Patrol, I already knew how to wear a uniform and how to march, and I had experienced room inspections during our summer encampments. Those experiences gave me confidence, but those first few weeks were still difficult.

My body ached from standing at attention and from the rigors of physical training. I was physically prepared, but the altitude at the Academy (7,258 feet above sea level) took its toll. Physical conditioning sessions were a daily routine, but they were designed to test more than our strength and stamina. An exercise station was not successfully completed until the entire team completed it to the cadre's satisfaction. We had to push and motivate each other. We learned to perform as a team. If one person fell out of a run, then we all paid the price. We learned quickly that we had to work together and support each other to survive.

Despite the focus on team efforts, you couldn't just blend in and disappear. There were specific opportunities to either excel or fail physically on your own during the first phase of training. I got my first opportunity to prove myself physically during our first physical fitness test (PFT). The PFT consists of pull-ups, a long jump, crunches, push-ups, and a 600-yard run. I scored 478 out of 500 total points, only missing a maximum score by seven seconds on the run. All the physical preparation I had done before coming to the Academy had paid off. I was determined to max the test the next time I took it so I could join the elite group of 500 club members, earning the maximum score of 500 points. I maxed out the test just a year later, achieving a feat accomplished by less than 5% of each graduating class. My name would eventually be mounted on a permanent display in the cadet gymnasium, joining my dad from the Class of 1970 in this achievement.

As we slowly transitioned from a group of individuals to a team, we prepared ourselves for the next phase of basic training in Jacks Valley, a 3,300-acre rural training area. The march out to Jacks Valley marked the beginning of the second phase of BCT, which pushed us to our limits, and then demanded more.

Once we arrived, we set up tents and filled countless sandbags to "harden" the area. The heat was oppressive, and we were covered in sweat and dirt. We learned teamwork and leadership skills on the Leadership Reaction Course. The course consisted of 12 timed obstacles that we had to solve as a team. We also learned stamina and determination on the dreaded Assault Course. This course also consisted of obstacles, but in addition, we low-crawled through mud, under barbed wire, and down hills while listening to pyrotechnic bombs going off in the distance. There was no option to quit or give up. Looking back, I would not say I relished my time in Jacks Valley, but I enjoyed the physical challenges and the camaraderie that came with it.

As I wrote letters home, my parents could see a transformation. The days of beauty pageants and cheerleading competitions were well behind me. My mom and dad later recalled how difficult it was to read those letters. My dad occasionally wondered, "Why couldn't she have gone to a normal college like her friends?" Then he would remind himself that I was pursuing a goal and doing what I wanted to do. My mom often got teary-eyed reading my letters and wondered what I had gotten myself into. She was both proud and scared at the same time.

In one of my letters, the reality of what I was training for set in:

> *I know that killing people and possibly dying for my country is part of my job, but I'm not looking forward to it. I think it would be a really difficult thing to do.*

I knew that risking my life and taking lives was part of this career of service I had chosen, especially if I planned to be a fighter pilot. It would be something I would have to come to grips with throughout my career.

At the end of our time in Jacks Valley, we marched back to join the cadet wing. We were exhausted, but proud of what we had accomplished during BCT. That night I wrote my parents a letter to share my thoughts:

> *Well, I'm back up on the hill now. We marched back this morning — it has been a very long and tiring day. Last night at the duty, honor, country briefing, they played the song, "I'm Proud to Be an American" and it gave me chills. It's hard to believe that I'm really in the Air Force and that I am going to be accepted into the Cadet Wing.*

We were finally accepted into the cadet wing to start our freshman year, also known as our "doolie" year. I had completed basic training, which could not be said of all my classmates. According to statistics released by the Air Force Academy, we started BCT with 1,164 cadets, and we finished basic training with 1,029 cadets. Not everyone makes it, and not everyone decides to stay. That was not an option for me; I had worked too hard to get here. The next morning, the Class of 1997 formed up in the center of the terrazzo and raised our right hands to take the Academy Honor Code oath:

> *We will not lie, steal, or cheat, nor tolerate among us anyone who does. Furthermore, I resolve to do my duty and to live honorably, so help me God.*

We were following in the footsteps of the first graduating class, the Class of 1959, who adopted the cadet honor code. This code would be something to live by and embrace during our four years at the Academy as we developed into leaders of character.

PROP AND WINGS

Shortly after being accepted into the cadet wing, I came back to my room one day and found a note on my desk.

Report to Harmon Hall. The Admissions Office wants to see you.

I was confused. What could they want at this point? I had never been to Harmon Hall before, the building where the superintendent, a three-star general in charge of the Academy, and his staff work. I made my way up the hill, nervous about finding my way into the headquarters building. After some wandering around, I finally found the admissions office. It was full of welcoming and smiling faces. My letters had made an impact, and they all wanted to meet the cadet who spent so much time writing letters to the Academy. I had proven that I could survive basic training, and now I just had to survive the rigors of the school year.

This first year was all about survival. We tried to be good at everything—academics, military activities, and athletics—but it was challenging. Every day was busy. We would wake up early to get into uniform and prepare for room inspection. Then at the appointed hour, we would make our way into the hallways in our cadet squadrons and call minutes, "There are 15 minutes until morning meal formation. Uniform of the day is blues. I say again . . ."

After breakfast, we would spend our mornings in academic classes, learning everything from the aerodynamic properties of a balsa wood airplane to computer programming. After morning classes, we formed up with our squadrons and marched to noon meal, which was no break. During lunch, upperclassmen would test our knowledge on current events. Lunch was followed by more classes. At the end of the academic day, we made our way down to the athletic fields for intramurals. After sports, we could grab dinner, then head back to our rooms for evening military training time and academic call to quarters. The day ended with taps, the final bugle call of the day. Time management was difficult, but I eventually found my routine to keep up with it all.

At the end of our freshman year, we would face the challenge of recognition, the formal finale of the fourth-class year when cadets are recognized as upper-class cadets. It was an acknowledgment that we had successfully met military training requirements and were ready for the next challenge. Recognition is essentially hell week in three days. It is demanding both physically and mentally and a reminder that we can't make it through alone. Recognition starts with intense physical training, everything from sprints to push-ups to low-crawl competitions. It ends with a Run to the Rock, a five-mile round-trip run to Cathedral Rock with the upper-class cadets, all designed to build teamwork and camaraderie.

Before recognition, as fourth-class cadets, we could not wear the coveted prop and wings (propeller and wings) device on our flight caps. As part of the ceremony at the end of recognition, we would pin the prop and wings on our uniforms. In addition to the prop and wings the upperclassmen presented to me, I got a package in the mail from my dad:

> Kim, I think these have rested long enough. I'm proud to have you wear them. Love, Dad.

In the envelope was a set of prop and wings worn by my dad when he was a cadet at the Air Force Academy. I was extremely proud to have made it through my first year, but I also knew there was still a long way to go.

EYE OF THE RABBIT

My fourth-class year was complete, but there were still many challenges ahead. Summers at the Academy were equally as intense as the academic year. One of the most worthwhile (and toughest) summer programs was SERE (Survival, Evasion, Resistance, and Escape). After spending four days in academic briefings, we were released into the wild in Saylor Park, a 26,000-acre training area within Pike National Forest. Initially, we had two instructors who taught us critical survival skills such as building shelters, making fires, scavenging for food, and making signaling devices.

One night, after several days without food, we found a rabbit in our camp. We were hungry and knew this was part of our survival test. When it came time to kill the rabbit, our instructor asked for volunteers. I decided to prove my toughness in the group of cadets and volunteered to kill the rabbit. It was horrifying, but I also understood that in a survival situation, you have to be able to overcome your fears. As tradition would have it at the time, one cadet would also be chosen to eat the rabbit's eyeball . . . pure protein, according to the instructors. We would not waste anything that could help us survive. When our instructor asked for volunteers, everyone looked at me once again.

"What the hell? How bad could it be?" I said to myself, more than anyone else.

I figured why not continue to prove my toughness in front of this group of male cadets. If I needed to survive in enemy territory, I wanted to prove I was tough enough to do it.

"Pop the eyeball in your mouth and swallow it, there's not much taste," my survival instructor said, encouraging me to do it quickly.

I promptly popped the eyeball into my mouth before I could change my mind. I shucked it down like an oyster and proudly kept it down. I earned praise and admiration for taking one for the team because nobody else wanted to do it.

The true test came when we departed our camp in teams of three to spend three days using our newly attained navigation skills to find checkpoints while aggressors, cadre simulating enemy personnel, hunted us down. Eventually, we got caught, and the "enemy" brought us to a mock prisoner of war camp where we would learn the skills of resistance training. It was miserable. We were held in solitary confinement without food or water for hours on end. The cells were dark and cold with loud music and enemy propaganda playing loudly over the speaker system, making it difficult to fall asleep. Occasionally we would hear footsteps coming down the hallway and knew they were pulling someone out for interrogation. Interrogations were the worst because you didn't want to say something you weren't supposed to. This was still training so they could not hurt us, as a real enemy might, but it was still miserable. And the worst part was being alone, separated from your teammates. When they finally brought us out of isolation, it was heartwarming to be with my classmates again. We were still in "captivity," but we knew we could get through it if we were together.

I am thankful to have gone through SERE training, knowing I had the training for a worst-case scenario. If I became a pilot and got shot down, then I would at least have the essential skills required to survive, evade capture, and resist pressure from the enemy. SERE showed us that we could endure tough times and work together as a team to persevere through challenges.

LIKE FATHER, LIKE DAUGHTER

Just before my final year at the Academy, I was interviewed and subsequently selected by a panel of cadets and officers to hold the position of

Cadet Wing Commander. The Cadet Wing Commander is responsible for all 4,000 cadets at the Air Force Academy, a position my dad held 25 years earlier. We were the first father-daughter wing commander duo in Academy history. My mom was proud, but not at all surprised. When interviewed by the local newspaper about us, she made the following comment, "It's very much like father, like daughter—very committed and very driven, but with a sense of concern for the people they're leading. And I think that's what makes them such good leaders."

It turns out that my liaison officer's prediction about me becoming a future cadet wing commander came true after all.

During parents' weekend, which happens every Labor Day weekend at the Air Force Academy, I had the opportunity to lead the entire cadet wing, all 4,000 cadets in a parade for the parents. To start the parade, we formed up on the terrazzo in the cadet area and then marched down the Bring Me Men ramp to the parade field. Parents would line the walkways to watch us march down. As I led the wing down the ramp, I remember one of the parents yelling out at me, "Look at you, young lady, leading all those men down the Bring Me Men ramp!"

It never occurred to me that this was ironic or unique. I was just doing my job leading the cadet wing. These types of comments would follow me throughout my career. I just never thought about it that way. I didn't see myself as a female Cadet Wing Commander, I was just the Cadet Wing Commander.

Leading my peers was challenging. I learned early on that you cannot please everyone as a leader and that you will often have to make unpopular decisions. But most significant, I learned the importance of sharing success and owning failure. On one occasion, half of our senior class was late to a dean's briefing. The dean oversaw academics, and he was also a one-star general officer. As you might guess, the proper military protocol would be to show up on time to a briefing with a general officer (or early to be completely accurate). It was my job to introduce the dean at the start of the briefing. Even though we were there at the start time, my classmates continued to come in late to the auditorium. It became so disruptive that we eventually shut the doors and took accountability. As a result of our disrespect to the one-star general, he restricted our entire class for the weekend. I decided I would own that decision and take responsibility for the actions of our class. It wasn't easy and I took some heat from my peers, but I learned early on that leaders have to make tough calls, enforce standards, and own their decisions. When our team does well, we celebrate their success, and when our team performs poorly or fails, then that's on us. As leaders, we own that failure. Yes, there may be several contributing factors, but in the end, the failure is ours. These were lessons that would serve me well throughout my career.

As Cadet Wing Commander, I also had the opportunity to work directly with the senior enlisted and senior officer leadership at the Academy. Chief Master Sergeant Lisa Robinson was a critical member of the team and worked with the cadet wing staff to teach us about upholding standards and personal accountability. Working with her also impressed on me the value of having a trusted advisor on your team to hold you accountable and give you honest feedback.

Brigadier General Stephen Lorenz was the Commandant of Cadets and my boss during my time as a Cadet Wing Commander. He certainly didn't hold back on giving me feedback and sharing his thoughts about leadership. We spent a lot of time together during Saturday morning wing inspections, better known as SAMIs (Saturday a.m. inspections). As we walked around monitoring the inspection process, General Lorenz would ask me questions about why we did things a certain way, such as, "Why do cadets fold t-shirts and underwear around cardboard so they can't be used?"

I didn't know the reason or purpose; that's just the way we did it. General Lorenz taught me a valuable lesson in those morning walks. We should continually evaluate why we do things. What is the purpose behind the training? I quickly realized the answer should not be "because we've always done it that way."

It became much clearer later in my career as I took command of new organizations and began asking why we do things a certain way. I came to realize that we should regularly evaluate why we do things and assess if there might be a better way. Just asking that question often means that we could find a better way of doing things and alleviate stress on the team. That thought process helped me focus on the team, find new ways to support them, improve their living and working conditions, and provide a more safe and secure working environment.

THE LONG BLUE LINE

I would never want to go through those four years again, but I would not have done it any other way. As graduation day approached, I was excited to begin the next adventure, but also sad to be leaving my friends behind. Wendy, Tara, Shannon, and Beth were my closest friends and allies. We supported each other during our respective lows and celebrated our achievements—we still do to this day. We share bonds that will last a lifetime because we survived this demanding time together.

Graduation week was an exciting time. It was the culmination of four difficult years at the Academy and a celebration of everything we had accomplished. Family, friends, and mentors came out for the event. On the morning of May 28, 1997, we had our commissioning ceremony where I would again take the oath of office and earn my lieutenant bars. I asked Major Donna Schutzius, my military arts and science instructor, to act as my commissioning officer. Since our commissioning officer would be the one to administer the oath of office, I wanted to select someone who had made a positive impact on me as a cadet. Major Schutzius wrote me a letter that morning with some words of advice that have stayed with me to this day:

> *Congratulations on all of your achievements—you have truly finished "this" race in first place! In examining your life [in 10–20 years] may contentment and peace fill your heart in knowing you were on the "right path." Please remember, Kim, no one can tell you what that "path" is for you. Only you can choose the path that is right for you!*

After the oath of office, my mom and dad came forward to pin on my second lieutenant bars. I felt a sense of pride, knowing I had accomplished what I set out to do. But I certainly didn't do it alone, and it was nice to celebrate with so many people who had helped me along the way. Later that day, I walked across the stage in Falcon Stadium and received my commission and diploma from the Secretary of Defense, William Cohen. It was an intense feeling of pride. I would graduate as a Distinguished Graduate with Academic, Athletic, and Military Distinction. I would finish number one in the military order of merit, earning the highest military performance average of all the cadets in my class, an achievement my dad

Figure 2.2   Graduation day with Wendy, Tara, and Shannon—friends who will last a lifetime. I remember feeling so much pride about what we had accomplished as well as excitement for the future.

also attained 27 years before when he graduated. Our graduating class totaled 797 new second lieutenants. We had started basic training with 1,164 cadets and graduated with 797. We lost 32% of our class over four years at the Academy. We were one of the smallest classes in recent history, but we had come together as a team. We would continue to support each other throughout our careers in the Air Force and beyond.

FROM CONCEPT TO CULTURE

The relationships and friendships I made at the Academy will last a lifetime. We went through tremendous challenges together and learned we could overcome them by working together and relying on each other for support when we needed it most. We didn't succeed as individuals; we met success as a team. Yes, it was a competitive environment, but we recognized we performed better by helping and encouraging each other. The Academy introduced us to the importance of the wingman concept, and we understood we should never leave a wingman behind. We committed to always being there to provide mutual support. However, we were only just beginning to appreciate the wingman concept, which was critical on the ground but even more so in the air.

Years later when I joined my first fighter squadron, I learned what it truly meant to be a good wingman. As fighter pilots, we do not fly alone; we always have the support of a wingman. According to Air Force Tactics, Techniques, and Procedures, "Wingmen are assigned the supporting role in the flight. Wingmen have visual lookout responsibilities and must maintain positional awareness throughout the flight. A wingman's duties are numerous and to do the job well, the wingman must understand the mission objectives and demonstrate personal discipline." During a mission, wingmen have a critical role to ensure the flight is safe. Wingmen are responsible for looking out for threats to the flight, either on the ground or in the air. Because a flight lead is focused on looking out for threats and targets in front of the flight, a wingman is responsible for checking the flight's six o'clock position, the area directly behind an aircraft where we can't see on our own. Wingmen provide critical mutual support and always "check six" for unseen threats.

As new fighter pilots, we went from having a basic understanding of the wingman concept to joining an elite team that fully embraced the wingman culture. "A distinct culture exists anytime a group of people are in consensus about how we do things around here and why."[2] In a fighter squadron, it was extremely clear—we knew how and why we did things. We fully grasped that the strength of the team was determined by the individuals who made up the team. From the newest wingman to the most experienced instructor, we came to know how each of us played a unique role on the team, how our individual contributions were critical for our shared success. If a teammate wasn't pulling their weight or wasn't making the cut, then it was our responsibility to help them meet standards, to raise their performance in order to elevate the performance of the team. I thrived in this environment. As a member of a fighter squadron, I knew the role I played and I felt valued for my contributions. The culture pushed me to perform at my best and help others excel. This wingman culture instilled in me a fighter pilot mindset and a fight for continuous improvement.

CONSIDERATIONS FOR LEADERS

Leaders own the responsibility for the culture of their teams. We must set the direction and make it a priority. To create and cultivate a wingman culture it is important for leaders to do the following:

- Clearly define roles and responsibilities for each team member.
- Reinforce why each team member's contribution is critical to shared success and how it relates to the bigger picture.
- Establish an environment of trust where team members can provide feedback without blame or shame.
- Foster an organizational belief in accountability, where we hold ourselves and others accountable to achieve higher levels of performance.

Leaders play a critical role in lifting team members to be their best possible selves to elevate the performance of the team. ***If you want to lead with courage, then create a wingman culture in your organization.***

Chapter 3

FIGHTER PILOT MINDSET

"The ultimate measure of a man is not where he stands in moments of comfort and convenience, but where he stands at times of challenge and controversy."

—Martin Luther King Jr.

Figure 3.1 My T-38 class at undergraduate pilot training. We would all go on to fly fighter or bomber aircraft in the Air Force.

When I started pilot training in 1999, there were 33 female fighter pilots in the Air Force, about 1% of fighter pilots. I knew I had a lot to prove, and so I put a lot of pressure on myself. I hated making mistakes. I was afraid of failing. I wish I knew then what I finally know now. Don't put so much pressure on yourself to get it perfect the first time. There will be plenty of mistakes and failures along the way. And when you fail, when you make mistakes—get up, dust yourself off, and give it another go.

CALLSIGN: "BAGS"

After two years at graduate school, I show up to undergraduate pilot training, newly married and ready to start my flying career. When I drive onto the base for the first time, I can see and hear a nonstop stream of aircraft flying overhead. I cannot wait to start, but I'm also nervous. I want to excel in pilot training so I can get my coveted fighter slot. I join my class of 30 students as we begin our journey at pilot training.

Before we can even get in the airplane, we have to get through academics and ground training, which includes the dreadful emergency procedures evaluations. To simulate the stress of an emergency, instructors put upgrading pilots in a demanding environment in the classroom. We stand in front of the class with our fellow pilots and other instructors watching and listening to everything we do. Instructors give us an emergency to handle and then we follow a prescribed mental model: maintain aircraft control, analyze the situation, take the proper action, and land as soon as conditions permit. It is uncomfortable to be put on the spot, but the ideal goal is to help us calmly respond in a stressful situation. We went through these simulated emergencies daily to help us prepare for the challenges of flight. And if we made a mistake, we would hear the dreaded words . . . "sit down." This meant sitting down and studying for the rest of the day. Ideally, we learned from our mistakes and got another chance the next day.

We eventually made our way through ground training, and it was finally time for our first flight in the mighty T-37 Tweet. The T-37 is a twin-engine trainer used for teaching the fundamentals of jet aircraft operation and for flying instruments, formation, and at night. Side-by-side seating in the T-37 makes it easier for an instructor to observe and communicate with a student. Its flying characteristics prepare students to transition to larger, faster aircraft in the future.

Walking out to our parking spot, I was feeling both excited and nervous. This was the next step on my journey to becoming a fighter pilot. The flight started well, but I started to feel nauseous partway through the flight. My instructor was demonstrating maneuvers to me, and I felt sick every time he took control of the airplane. To my dismay, I got actively airsick on almost every flight for the first several weeks of flying. It was miserable. I should not have been surprised since I got carsick as a kid, didn't like spinning rides at the county fair, and had a few airsickness episodes while flying Cessnas. Maybe it's shocking I still wanted to be a fighter pilot, but I figured airsickness was something I could get past. I tried everything. I ate bananas, chewed ginger snaps before every flight (I still can't eat ginger cookies to this day), wore motion sickness bracelets . . . you name it, I tried it. I wanted this so badly that I was willing to try anything and kept pressing on despite the insecurity I was feeling. *Could I actually make it through this?*

Air sickness is not uncommon for new pilots, and the Air Force has their own methods of getting student pilots over motion sickness. The Bárány chair, which looks like a large metal hula-hoop with a seat in the middle, spins around to stimulate ear-fluid movement. The intent is to correct motion sickness by helping the inner ear adjust to certain movements.

The chair was named for Robert Bárány, a Hungarian physiologist who researched the vestibular system in the early 20th century. The chair has been used to help pilots overcome motion sickness for years. But I still think it's a torture device. There's nothing quite like spinning around in a chair with your head down to induce tumbling sensations to get your inner ear used to the movement. Despite the discomfort, I committed to trusting the process. I had to get through this if I had any chance of becoming a fighter pilot.

Initially, we don't receive an overall unsatisfactory for airsickness on a flight, but after several flights, if we continue to get sick, we will be graded as unsatisfactory overall, meaning we failed the flight. After we have enough unsatisfactory flights, we go through progress checks with leadership, and eventually, we face an elimination ride. Luckily, my body adapted, and I got over my airsickness before being kicked out of the program. I also managed to get my very first call sign in the Air Force because of my airsickness issues: Bags. (I used more than a few airsickness bags during my time in the T-37.) Getting airsick was miserable, but persevering was worth it in the long run because I really wanted to be a pilot. To this day, I still prefer being at the controls. If I have control, then my body knows what is about to happen, and the motion doesn't bother me.

PRESSURE TO CONFORM

After about six months of academics and flying in the T-37, it was time to select our next path. Our options were the fighter/bomber track flying the T-38 Talon, the airlift/tanker track flying the T-1 Jayhawk, or leaving Columbus Air Force Base for the helicopter track, flying the TH-1H Huey at Fort Rucker, Alabama. I knew I wanted to go fighters from day one and that hadn't changed despite my initial problems with airsickness. I had done well enough on academics and my check rides to earn a spot at the top of my class.

The T-38 environment was exciting. The T-38 is a twin-engine, high-altitude, supersonic jet trainer with tandem seating on rocket-powered ejection seats. I was finally surrounded by fighter pilots who would teach me the art of flying aerobatics, formation, night, instrument, and low-level navigation training.

My first flight in the T-38, also known as the dollar ride, was awesome. I was hooked. After the dollar ride, the tradition was that you would present your IP (instructor pilot) with a dollar. Since it is supposedly impossible to fail your first flight and nothing in life is free, students give their instructor a decorated dollar bill after the flight to "pay them back" for the ride. Well, after looking at several of the dollar bills given previously, I quickly realized the tradition also involved giving your instructor a dollar bill decorated with pornography. That was not my thing, but I decided to play the game in my own way. Instead of buying a *Playboy* magazine to cut out pictures of nude women, I decided to buy a *Playgirl* magazine and cut out pictures of nude men. After the flight, I gave the dollar to my IP and when he flipped it over, he almost fell out of his chair. He laughed and yelled across the room, "You gotta be freaking kidding me."

I had a good laugh, too. Was it the right thing to do? Maybe not, but it worked for me at the time. Looking back, maybe I should have helped change the culture then, but as one of the only women, I just wanted to do my best in the airplane and not invite other distractions.

Women were first admitted to pilot training in 1976, but because of existing policies, their flying was limited to non-combat roles. Congress removed the legal ban on women in combat aircraft in December 1991, but the Department of Defense policy still prohibited women from taking up combat aircraft assignments until the policy ban was lifted by Secretary of Defense Les Aspin in April 1993. Numbers have improved since my pilot training days, but according to Headquarters Air Force, there are still only 124 female fighter pilots of the 3,818 fighter pilots serving in the Air Force (as of June 2022).

Thankfully, "dollar ride" payments are much cleaner these days. The flying community, particularly the fighter community, has made significant changes to what is acceptable and appropriate behavior in the flying squadron. As a Colonel flying in a fighter squadron with significant combat experience and credibility, I had no problem stepping up to let people know if they had crossed the line. Most don't cross the line anymore, and if they do, there are other pilots willing to step up first before I do because they respect me for who I am and what I have done in the airplane.

LET IT GO

Most of my flights in the T-38 went well. However, I did manage to completely botch my last formation check ride. On a formation flight, we take off with two aircraft and perform maneuvers close to each other. My flight started out all right, but the visor on my helmet fogged up while we were in tight formation. It was uncomfortable for me being that close to another airplane when I couldn't clearly see all of the features used to ensure we are in the right position. I moved away from the other airplane and told my evaluating check pilot in the backseat about the issue. He took the airplane, told me to clean the visor, and then move back into formation. I quickly did what I could to fix the issue, but I was also worried I had bombed the flight for not flying in tight formation. And because I couldn't get that off my mind, I continued to make more errors. It was the worst flight I had ever flown, and it was my fault because I couldn't compartmentalize. I let my concern spin out of control and get the best of me.

I received several downgrades on that flight and was worried it would eliminate my chances of getting the fighter I wanted. However, that mission was also a powerful lesson for me, and I am thankful it happened early in my flying career. If you screw up, learn the lesson, don't do it again, and MOVE ON. We can spend too much time critiquing ourselves and worrying about the mistakes we make. In reality, we can perform better if we internalize the error, commit to not letting it happen again, and then let it go. We can't spend precious time thinking about the past 30 seconds. Rather, we need to constantly be thinking about the next 30 seconds to stay ahead of the jet.

Luckily, I had performed well enough on my flights that I still finished toward the top of my class, but I know I could have done better. Even though I look at that check ride as a failure, it helped me succeed in the end. Sometimes failures in life can lead to even greater success in the future.

IT'S TOO LATE NOW!

As pilot training came to a close, it was time to start thinking about the airplane I wanted to fly. We were able to submit our dream sheet with the airplane we desired, and our flight commander would choose the aircraft based on our performance. I learned flying formation was not overly exciting to me, but flying low-level missions was something I enjoyed. We also spent time talking to pilots of fighter and bomber airplanes to see what they liked most about their airplanes and missions. I realized there was something about the A-10 that appealed to me. I liked the mission of close air support, being able to support our troops on the ground and ensure they could get home safely to their families. That was something I believed in and wanted to be a part of. However, at the same time, my husband was already flying the A-10. *Should I go into the same career field as him?* He was already established in flying the airplane. Would I constantly be compared to him? There was no precedent I was aware of for a husband-and-wife team in the same airplane. We talked about other airplanes and how it would work with joint spouse assignments. We knew at some point we wanted to be able to live together and have kids. There weren't any comparable examples for us to follow, so we decided to make the best decision we could with the information we had.

Assignment night at pilot training was exciting. At Columbus Air Force Base, it was standard protocol for the assignment night festivities to be held at the Officer's Club (better known as the O-Club). On assignment night, students and instructors pack the venue for the event. It's an exhilarating night and everyone wants to be part of it. To find out our assignment, we reported on stage with our back to a large screen that flashed pictures of different aircraft. When it was my turn, I got on stage, and my flight commander announced I would be flying the A-10. I was ecstatic!

Figure 3.2 Pilot training graduation with my parents and my brother, Alex. I don't think I ever could have imagined the path my life would take when my parents pinned on my pilot wings.

Out of seven students in my T-38 flight, there was only one A-10, and I couldn't have been happier. As I walked back to my seat and sat down, I turned around to look at my husband.

"You sure this is okay?" I asked.

He smiled and laughed, "It's too late now!"

WORK HARD, PLAY HARD

After pilot training, I reported to Randolph Air Force Base in Texas for Introduction to Fighter Fundamentals (IFF). IFF is an eight-week course designed to transform newly graduated pilots selected to fly fighters into fighter pilot wingmen. We were now flying the AT-38B, which was like the T-38 I flew during pilot training, only now we had a gunsight and a practice bomb dispenser. During the short course, we learned critical tactical flying skills like BFM (basic fighter maneuvers) and surface attack. BFM missions were our first opportunity to "fight" against another aircraft. We learned how to use angles to enter an opponent's turn circle so we could get our nose on them and shoot them down. We also learned some basic bombing skills using practice bombs on the training ranges. It was not enough training to feel good at any of it, but it allowed us to have a brief introduction before we started the next phase of training.

During our time at IFF, we began to understand what it meant to be a fighter pilot and to have a fighter pilot mindset. Legendary fighter pilot and ace General Robin Olds described what it meant to him: "Fighter pilot is an attitude. It is cockiness. It is aggressiveness. It is self-confidence. It is a streak of rebelliousness, and it is competitiveness. But there's something else—there is a spark. There is the desire to be good. To do well in the eyes of your peers, and in your own mind." Good fighter pilots are teachable, and they have a commitment to excellence through accountability. Although not officially defined, a fighter pilot mindset centers on the desire to constantly strive for improvement while taking ownership of the process and learning from our mistakes. Over time, fighter pilots have learned the only way to get to the level of high performance expected is through deliberate progress and a constant review and analysis of our performance. Nobody wants to make mistakes or fail. And fighter pilots? We tend to be our own worst critics. We put a lot of pressure on ourselves to get it right the first time. But a perfect flight? A perfect mission? Near impossible. So, we focus on holding ourselves accountable, learning from mistakes, and sharing those lessons learned with others to elevate the performance of the team.

We also learned what it took to be a good lieutenant in the squadron when we were not flying. We learned to make coffee first thing when we came in at 0500 for morning flights. We also acquired the art of making jalapeño popcorn, a critical ingredient to any fighter squadron. A good batch can make you cry and cough at the same time. Every Friday meant time in the squadron bar listening to war stories and sharing shots of Jeremiah Weed. Not many people drink Jeremiah Weed for the taste. A single shot can make your throat burn and your stomach feel like it's on fire. This was only an introduction to fighter pilot culture, but it would prepare us for stepping foot into our very first fighter squadron.

We all lived on base for our eight-week stint at IFF, which meant we could easily walk from our dorm rooms to the Officer's Club on base. The Auger Inn is in the basement of the club, and for good reason, since the other customers may not want to witness the shenanigans that occur at the bar on any given Friday night. The Auger Inn takes its name from the aviation term *auger in*, meaning to crash catastrophically. Fighter pilots often use gallows humor to talk about crashing; it takes the edge off the serious nature of what we do.

During the week, we worked hard, and we endured a significant amount of stress, so Friday night was our night to blow off steam. We had many good nights at the Auger Inn, with likely too much alcohol consumed, but we were lieutenants and soon-to-be fighter pilots, and we thought we were invincible. It was at the Auger Inn where I first learned the fighter pilot game called "Dead Bug," or Deceased Insect as most fighter pilots refer to it. On any given Friday night, you could hear the phrase "Dead Bug" being yelled in the bar. In an instant, every fighter pilot in the room would drop to the floor on their backs with feet and legs in the air, beer flying and stools crashing around them. The slowest to make their way to the floor would risk having to buy the next round of beer. Perhaps silly and childish, it was also fun and hilarious to see pilots of all ranks crashing to the floor at a single command. Although there are plenty of critics of squadron bars, there is quite a bit of learning that goes on in a fighter bar on Friday nights. War stories get going after a few beers and the reality is, we all learn something from those stories. We learn from others' mistakes, experiences, and failures.

On one Friday afternoon, we got a visit from Major Rob "Sweetness" Sweet, an A-10 pilot who had combat experience in Desert Storm. He also spent time as a prisoner of war after his A-10 was shot down by enemy fire. Sweetness's briefing stuck with me because he described what it was like to fly the A-10 after receiving battle damage and shared stories of his time in captivity. I was impressed by his ability to share the details in such a matter-of-fact way to help us learn from his experiences. He also relayed stories from other A-10 pilots about flying in manual reversion, the A-10s back-up flight control system. He talked about where they succeeded and where they failed. I had no idea at the time how important these war stories would be in helping me navigate my own combat experiences later in my career.

The sharing of lessons learned is part of the fighter pilot mindset because we want to help make the team better. When we have the courage to be vulnerable and share our stories, both good and bad, even when they expose mistakes or weaknesses, our experiences can help make other people better. We would face many failures in training and sometimes in combat, too, but the intent was that we would learn from them and then share them with other pilots. We had to learn to fail forward.

FAILING FORWARD MINDSET

I learned some powerful lessons during my flight training as a result of struggles and mistakes. However, I also spent a lot of time critiquing myself and worrying about my mistakes when they happened. I was worried about what people would think. I was worried about not living up to expectations. The reality is, we all make mistakes. We all fail. It's not if, but when. Therefore, we need to learn to fail forward. We can do this best by having a growth mindset instead of a fixed mindset.

Dr. Carol Dweck, the author of *Mindset: The New Psychology of Success*, talks about the importance of having a growth mindset: "The passion for stretching yourself and sticking to it, even (or especially) when it's not going well, is the hallmark of the growth mindset. This is the mindset that allows people to thrive during some of the most challenging times in their lives."[1] She goes on to explain the benefits of having a growth mindset when faced with failure: "Even in the growth mindset, failure can be a painful experience. But it doesn't define you. It's a problem to be faced, dealt with, and learned from."[2]

With a fixed mindset, however, Dweck explains, you will want to prove yourself correct and avoid looking deficient rather than learning from your mistakes. Those with fixed mindsets are likely going to avoid challenges and experiences where they might fail. And by doing so, they lose the opportunity to grow and improve.

It took me some time to shift from a fixed mindset to a growth mindset during flight training. Making mistakes and failing was painful. But the reality was, the instructors were also looking to see how we reacted when we failed. Could we learn from those mistakes and strive to be better? I became a better pilot and leader by working through those difficult experiences. If you allow it, failure can lead to growth and success.

EMBRACING RISK

Later in my career, I got a real test of leading a team through failure. The 422 Test and Evaluation Squadron (TES) at Nellis Air Force Base in Las Vegas, Nevada, has a unique mission. Before any aircraft hardware or software is accepted and released to operational fighter squadrons, it is first tested by the 422 TES. In addition to operational testing, the squadron is also responsible for the development and testing of new tactics, techniques, and procedures. There is always a long list of requests to upgrade aircraft on both the hardware and software side, and these lists get prioritized according to funding.

When the Air Force decided to upgrade the A-10 from the A-10A to the A-10C, the A-10 jumped to the top of that funding and priority list. This extensive upgrade, involving both hardware and software, meant that the A-10 would be transitioning from executing tactics with 1970s technology to executing new tactics with state-of-the-art precision weapons. Think of it like transitioning from a rotary phone to a smartphone. It was a much-needed upgrade that would bring us up-to-date with the technology of our sister fighter units. This was an important mission, and we knew we had to get it right.

Daily, we made micro-level tactical decisions in software design and development. In the broader sense, these decisions affected how we would fly and execute missions in the long term. During our testing of the A-10, we knew we had to take risks to improve, but sometimes that meant failing. The process was hard and often painful.

A few years into my assignment, I became the director of the A-10 Division, and I got the opportunity to lead a contingent of pilots, engineers, and analysts to Florida so we could test out our newly updated weapons system software. We had put a lot of work into making the adjustments, and now it was time to go to the range to test our air-to-air weapons. We did all the preliminary testing, and everything looked good. To test the missiles, we paid to have high-tech, full-size drones airborne so we could shoot our missiles and see how they performed. We had several analysts on the ground using high-tech systems to watch and evaluate our performance. We got airborne uneventfully, rejoined with the drones, and set up to execute the live missile test. It was a beautiful blue-sky day, and I eventually maneuvered to get the drone right in the center of my heads-up display. I locked onto the drone. I checked all my parameters and settings.

"Ready, Ready, Fox," I declared over the radio.

I pressed down on the weapons release button to fire the missile.

Nothing. Absolutely nothing happened. The missile stayed on the rail. All those assets, people, money . . . and the missile stayed on the rail. Talk about a letdown.

It turned out that in our testing we missed one critical step in the software. While trying to do something new that would make it easier for pilots to shoot the missiles, we initially made it worse. Now it didn't work at all. Back to the drawing board. In the end, we got the system working and found the best possible solution. This was neither the first time nor the last time we made mistakes in the transition from the A-10A to the A-10C, but we learned and moved forward after each one.

Beyond testing the new airplane, we also played a key role in taking our show on the road. We regularly traveled to A-10 units throughout the world to show A-10 pilots the latest technology and talk about how to train pilots with the new equipment. As an A-10 community, we prided ourselves on being experts in our aging technology, and now we were transitioning to a completely unfamiliar environment of smart weapons. We had been executing tactics one way for so long, and now we were being asked to do something completely new, different, and outside of our comfort zone. We were all motivated and driven to succeed, but it was challenging to change the way we operated as an A-10 community.

Our younger pilots seemed to transition with ease, but for those of us who had been around longer, the transition was a lot harder. In the end, even the old hats came around because they realized that it was a better way of executing and doing business. Getting these older pilots to come around was the conceptual shift necessary to get traction with these changes. We made every effort to ensure we could still do the basics, but we also had to stay current with the latest technology. We established an environment of trust in the A-10 community and the 422 pilots were respected for what we had done to improve the airplane. Change wasn't easy, and there were risks in altering the way we operated. Eventually, we realized those risks would also help us to improve our capabilities and make us more effective and efficient in the airplane. We didn't always get it right as we developed and tested the A-10C, we had plenty of small failures along the way, but ultimately, we learned from those errors and found a better way forward.

We will inevitably make mistakes and fail on our leadership journey, and our teammates will observe how we respond in difficult moments. Failure is a real possibility when we push ourselves to try new things and get outside our comfort zones. If we are going to achieve a high level of performance, then we must embrace smart risk. When we set the example, our team will follow because they know it is safe to do so. General Jim Mattis, former Secretary of Defense, explained a comparable approach in his book, *Call Sign Chaos*. "If a commander expects subordinates to seize fleeting opportunities under stress, his organization must reward this behavior in all facets of training, promoting, and commending. More important, he must be tolerant of mistakes. If the risk takers are punished, then you will retain in your ranks only the risk averse."[3] Mistakes will be made, so we need to encourage our team to acknowledge and learn from them. If we want the lower levels of our organization to think innovatively and be prepared to take risks, the example needs to come from the top. Failure may feel devastating, but we can't have innovative success without it.

CONSIDERATIONS FOR LEADERS

To be effective in a rapidly changing environment, leaders must create a culture focused on continuous improvement where there is a desire to excel and be the best at what we do. So, how do we cultivate this fighter pilot mindset in our organizations?

- Be intentional about analyzing performance. Shift away from a mindset that failure results in punishment.
- Inspire teammates to get outside their comfort zones and try new things. Reward innovative ideas and smart risk-taking.
- Highlight the positive aspects of mistakes and failure by focusing on the lessons learned and what will be done differently the next time.
- Encourage team members to embrace vulnerability by sharing their experiences so that others can develop and grow.

By inspiring this fighter pilot mindset within our team, we can thrive during stressful experiences and foster innovation and creativity. It's okay for us to fail, but we need to fail forward . . . to fail *and* learn from what we did wrong. ***If you want to lead with courage, then adopt a fighter pilot mindset and learn to fail forward.***

Chapter 4

PREPARE, PRACTICE, PLAN FOR CONTINGENCIES

"Luck is what happens when preparation meets opportunity."
—Seneca

Figure 4.1 I found my passion and my purpose in flying the
A-10 Warthog and supporting our troops on the ground.
Photo credit: Airman First Class Kristine Legate

THE A-10 WARTHOG

In 1970, when the request for a close air support platform came about,
US policy was shifting away from a nuclear deterrence option as the sole
means of stopping a Warsaw Pact invasion of Central Europe. As a result,
the military was looking for conventional ways to destroy hordes of Soviet
tanks massed in positions throughout Eastern Europe. Based on plans for
tank-on-tank battles, the aircraft design team decided to build an airplane
around a 19-foot-long 30 mm Gatling gun that could kill enemy tanks.
Head of the team, Dr. Robert Sanitor, said, "We literally sat down and
designed a plane around the gun we had to have."[1] The book *Warthog*
describes the preliminary specifications for an ideal close air support platform:

1. The plane has to be able to operate out of short, primitive
   airfields.
2. It should be reliable and easy to maintain in the field under
   wartime conditions.

3. It must be able to carry a large amount of ordnance and specifically must be able to kill tanks and armor.
4. It must have sufficient range to loiter "on call" near the battlefield, and when needed for CAS [close air support] it should have enough remaining endurance to find the target, identify and confirm that it is indeed enemy, rather than friendly, and then destroy it.
5. It must fly at least 350 knots but be maneuverable enough to turn tightly over the battlefield so that the pilot will not lose sight of the target when visibility is low.
6. It must be survivable; it should be able to take damage from ground fire and still return to base with a healthy pilot.
7. It should be a low-cost airplane in comparison to prices being quoted for supersonic jet fighters, and cost overruns were not to be allowed.[2]

The A-10 Thunderbolt II (more affectionately known as the Warthog) was the first Air Force aircraft specifically designed for close air support of ground forces. The A-10 offers remarkable maneuverability at low airspeeds and low altitude and is a highly accurate weapons-delivery platform. It can loiter over the target area for extended periods and carries 16,000 pounds of weapons on 11 stations underneath the airplane. The 30 mm Gatling gun is capable of shooting 3,900 rounds per minute. The A-10 may not be sleek or sexy or all that high-tech, but it performs close air support missions like no other aircraft.

According to military doctrine, close air support, or CAS, is a critical element of joint fire support that requires detailed planning, coordination, and training of ground and supporting air forces for safe and effective execution. CAS is officially defined as "air action by aircraft against hostile targets that are in close proximity to friendly forces and that require detailed integration of each air mission with the fire and movement of those forces."[3] CAS is a necessary mission to effectively support our troops on the ground.

As requested, the Warthog was designed to be survivable. The flight controls were all built with redundant systems with manual backups. The fuel tanks were enclosed in protective foam lining to prevent fire after battle damage. The A-10 also has two remarkably reliable engines. Perhaps most loved by its pilots, the cockpit is surrounded by what is affectionately called the titanium bathtub. The pilot literally sits inside thick slabs of titanium armor shaped like a bathtub to protect the cockpit and aircraft systems, enabling it to absorb a significant amount of damage and continue flying. The A-10 may be ugly, but it is a tough airplane, and it was built to take some hits while performing its mission. I did not know how important the survivable design of the airplane would be for me while performing the CAS mission.

ON HOG DRIVING

I was extremely excited to arrive at Davis-Monthan Air Force Base in Tucson, Arizona, to begin my A-10 training. I couldn't wait to get started. We had several weeks of academics and flights in the simulator before we could get in the airplane. There are no two-seat versions of the A-10 (except the one prototype on display) so the first flight in an A-10 is solo. Our instructor would follow us closely throughout the mission, but it was still a single-seat fighter jet, and we would be on our own. We had to be ready.

We prepared by taking weeks of academics, studying aircraft systems and procedures. We also practiced by flying missions in our aircraft simulators. We repeatedly went through our checklists and procedures. And finally, we planned for contingencies by going through emergency procedure simulations. We talked about worst-case scenarios and our responses in the event of an emergency. Preparing, practicing, and planning for contingencies was an integral part of our training before we could even get into the airplane.

THE ART OF CHAIR FLYING

I never felt like a natural pilot, so I had to work hard, and it paid off. By using a pilot's preparation technique called chair flying, I could visualize and practice for a mission in advance. Every night before I flew, I would sit in a chair in my room facing a diagram of the cockpit on the wall. I would then talk through every part of my mission, practicing radio calls, thinking through maneuver parameters, and analyzing potential areas that could go wrong on the mission. Chair flying essentially meant I got a free mission to practice before I ever got into the airplane. And on this free mission, I was the sole evaluator. I could find my weaknesses and study harder or practice more so when it came time for the actual mission, I was better prepared.

The concept of chair flying is something I employed to prepare myself for flying missions, but I have also used the technique in many situations in my personal and professional life. If we chair fly a stressful situation we anticipate at work or at home, we can prime ourselves for action, effectively cope with stress, and create a positive outcome. Studies about the psychology of fear tell us that repeated exposure to similar situations leads to familiarity. And familiarity reduces the likelihood of becoming stressed or fearful of what could happen.

Dr. Anders Ericsson, a cognitive psychologist and author of the book *Peak: Secrets from the New Science of Expertise*, is internationally recognized as a researcher regarding expertise and human performance. His work reveals the importance of deliberate and purposeful practice in order to become an expert. He pinpoints what sets expert performers apart from everyone else as the "quality and quantity of their mental representations"— the mental images we develop during deliberate practice. Ericsson goes on to say that "through years of practice, [experts] develop highly complex and sophisticated representations of the various situations they are likely to encounter in their fields. These representations allow them to make faster, more accurate decisions and respond more quickly and effectively in a given situation. This, more than anything else, explains the difference in performance between novices and experts."[4]

Chair flying enables us to practice, develop appropriate mental images, and visualize our success. It empowers us to visualize how we will overcome obstacles that might get in the way of our success so we can achieve a high level of performance. It also equips us with the courage to fail because, in practice or training, we can try new things and take smart risks. We can expand what we think we can do. We will know what works and what doesn't. If we're not making mistakes or failing in training, then we need to ask ourselves, are we challenging ourselves enough? Do we have a growth mindset, or do we have a fixed mindset where we're less likely to try new things? When we stretch ourselves in practice or training and get outside our comfort zones, then we are better prepared to face those critical moments in execution. Training and preparation can be the antidote to fear. When we are prepared, fear is reduced. As we prepare, we become competent, and when we are competent, we become more confident.

FLYING THE WARTHOG

After a month of ground training, it is finally time for my first flight in the A-10. As we walk out onto the blazing hot tarmac with the summer sun beating down, I am excited and nervous to fly the fearsome A-10. But I also feel ready for this moment. My crew chief is standing at attention next to the airplane and salutes me as I approach. I return his salute, shake his hand, and give him my saddlebags and helmet bag. The saddlebags contain checklists and maps of our training areas. I take my time doing the preflight inspection, looking over the airplane to make sure everything complies with the checklist. Before climbing up the ladder, I zip up my G-suit and fasten my harness. My crew chief follows me up the ladder, strapping me into the ejection seat so I am locked in tight in case I have to eject. I start the engines and go through the preflight checks with my crew chief, checking all the systems to make sure everything is working properly. I signal to my crew chief that it's time to pull chocks (blocks placed against an aircraft's wheels to prevent it from moving) and taxi out to the end of the runway. I can barely contain my excitement, but I am also feverishly making sure I haven't missed anything. The crew chiefs do their last checks in the arming area and give us a thumbs up signaling we are good to go. I make my way onto the runway with my instructor following close behind me so he can watch everything I am doing. The radio crackles, "Lobo 06, cleared for takeoff."

I push both throttles forward with my left hand then release the brakes, moving my heels to the floor of the airplane to control the rudder pedals with my feet. I barrel down the runway, checking my airspeed and engine gauges to ensure they are within limits. Then at 135 knots (or 155 miles per hour), I gently pull back on the stick with my right hand, allowing the airplane to lift off the ground. I lean forward to grab the gear handle, raise the gear, then use the flap lever to put the flaps up. Within seconds, I am flying at 230 miles per hour. *I am finally airborne in the A-10.* I have about a second to enjoy the moment, and then it's time to get to work.

We had about ten flights in the A-10 doing instrument work and learning about aircraft performance before they finally let us go to the range to shoot the gun. The GAU-8 30 mm Avenger is a seven-barrel Gatling gun that fires approximately 70 rounds per second. The gun was legendary, and everyone was eager to go to the range for the first time. We're not *really* considered to be an A-10 pilot until we shoot the gun. As we make our way to the Barry M. Goldwater range in the Arizona desert for my first Basic Surface Attack mission, I am excited and nervous. I want to be good at this. After all, hitting the target is a critical component to being a good A-10 pilot.

We arrive on the range and check out the area to make sure I know where the target is and how we will maneuver in a rectangular pattern for practice passes. With my instructor tucked in behind me to ensure I'm doing it right, I roll in on the target for the first time. The first pass is dry, meaning I won't actually shoot anything; it is intended for getting the mechanics right. I start my roll-in to the target at 6,000 feet above the ground and 1.7 miles from the target to ensure I am at a 30-degree dive angle. After demonstrating I can get the parameters right, it is time for my first hot pass. My instructor radios the range control officer to let him know we are going hot.

"Two's in," I say as confidently as possible, letting the range controller know I am rolling in on the target.

I roll in to point the nose of my airplane directly at the target (a metal container designed to look like a tank). I stabilize the airplane, fine-tune my aimpoint, and pull the trigger. I immediately hear the roar of the cannon as the jet shakes violently below me. I smell the gun gasses and see the smoke in front of my cockpit. Then, most impressively, I see sparkles as my bullets hit the target below. I immediately start a steep climb, pulling Gs (G forces) to get away from the ground in what we call a safe escape maneuver. It is awesome!

My favorite thing about the A-10 is the 30 mm Gatling gun. It is incredibly precise, which is the reason it also happens to be our go-to weapon of choice in a troops-in-contact situation where precision is required to ensure the safety of our ground troops. Once we got good at firing the gun on the conventional range, we moved to firing on the tactical range where ground troops are involved. We learn quickly that accuracy is critical and could be the difference between life and death for our troops on the ground. Preparation is non-negotiable.

A NATION AT WAR

On the morning of September 11, 2001, I was in crew rest for a night-flying mission. To fly at night, Air Force regulations require a pilot to have crew rest (12 hours between official duties with the opportunity for at least eight hours of uninterrupted rest). Just before 6:00 a.m., the phone rang. I was surprised that one of my classmates would be calling at that hour.

"Kim, turn on the TV," I heard him yell through the phone.

I turned on the TV just in time to see the second plane hit the World Trade Center. After watching the events unfold, I knew we were under attack. I also knew my life as an A-10 pilot and my career as an Air Force officer was about to change dramatically. I called my parents to make sure they were watching and to let them know I was safe on the base.

Davis-Monthan Air Force Base immediately went to THREATCON DELTA, which meant they shut down the base for everyone. You could not get in or out. According to the Department of Defense, Threat Condition Delta (now known as Force Protection Condition Delta) applies in the immediate area where a terrorist attack has occurred or when intelligence has been received of a likely terrorist action against a specific location or person. Our commander recalled everyone into the squadron. We had no idea what was going to happen or what our response would be. As we watched the news, the severity of the attack sunk in. Many of the pilots in our squadron had friends and family who were airline pilots or worked in the Pentagon. This felt personal.

I think we all knew that we would be going to war; it was just a matter of time. Terrorists had attacked our homeland, and there would be a response. It was impressive to see our nation come together, to know we had taken a huge blow, but we would fight back. We would find the people who did this and act. We, of course, were at the receiving end of these orders, but we still speculated about what we might do and when we might go. Little did I know that only a few months later, my squadron would start spinning up for our deployment to support the Global War on Terrorism.

THE JET DOESN'T KNOW THE DIFFERENCE

I finished my A-10 training in December 2001 and moved to Pope Air Force Base in North Carolina to join the ranks of the elite 75th Fighter Squadron and 23rd Fighter Group, whose heritage was legendary. It was the first US combat group to be formed in a combat zone during World War II and inherited the mission of the disbanded American Volunteer Group, known as the Flying Tigers. Its P-40 aircraft carried the standard shark's mouth marking, which was thought to intimidate enemies and is still used on 23rd Fighter Group aircraft today.[5] There was something about flying A-10s with those shark teeth; everyone wanted to be a part of the famous Flying Tigers.

I was both excited and nervous walking into the 75th Fighter Squadron on day one. I knew I would need to prove myself, just as every new fighter pilot is expected to do. I also knew that I would be the only female pilot in the fighter squadron. I intended to work hard and have a good attitude. It didn't matter if I was male or female—I would be judged, just as every young wingman is judged. I did my best to just think of myself as a new wingman coming into a squadron that had to prove themselves. I had thick skin, I could take feedback, and I would work hard to improve where I had weaknesses. I vowed to show up to every mission as ready and prepared as I could.

Over time, I came to look at the guys in my squadron as my brothers. They watched out for me and respected me for my credibility in the airplane. I was performing well in my mission qualification training, so I quickly found my place in this male-dominated community. After I completed my mission qualification training, I was officially combat-ready, meaning I could deploy with the squadron when the time came. Now, I really felt like an A-10 pilot and a member of the squadron. But there was still another rite of passage . . . the naming ceremony. Fighter pilots normally get their call signs at a naming ceremony after they achieve combat mission ready status. A call sign can be based on something stupid you've done in the airplane or a play on your name or personality (think Maverick or Goose from *Top Gun*). And once a pilot flies with the call sign in combat, it's their call sign for life.

On this night, we gathered in the bar to name all the newest pilots in the squadron. When it was my turn to get named, I had to leave the room while the other pilots told stories about me and came up with ideas for my call sign. Stories only have to be 10% true, so I had no idea what I was going to walk back into. I came back into the bar to cheers of approval from the other pilots as they announced my new call sign. From here on out, I would be known as Killer Chick or KC for short.

It turns out, my gender didn't really matter. The jet doesn't know the difference. And my team didn't care about the difference either; the guys in my squadron just cared that I could perform in the airplane.

Figure 4.2 My call sign, Killer Chick, stayed with me throughout my career in the Air Force, although most people just called me KC.

PREPARING FOR POTHOLES

Over time I realized the more prepared I was for missions, the more confident I was in my skills and ability to meet challenges. Preparation positioned me to face any doubts or uncertainty I was feeling. Facing my fears came down to preparation, practice, and planning for contingencies. The more prepared I was, the less nervous I felt about what was to come. Preparing to do hard things made me better at doing hard things.

First, before a mission, I prepared by studying my aircraft systems and knowing the enemy's threat systems. I knew what would happen when systems on the aircraft failed or what defensive techniques worked against our enemy's threat systems. I studied and reviewed the data. I did my homework. After I prepared for a mission, I took it a step further, and I practiced. The night before a mission, or even the morning of, I would think through the flight and visualize our plan of action. As a result, I felt more confident jumping into the airplane. Finally, I planned for contingencies, mentally preparing for what could go wrong. I didn't just think through what happened when everything was going right, I also thought about what to do when things went wrong. It's a good thing to be optimistic and focus on a positive outcome, but it's also important to look ahead at the potholes down the road. *Where can things go wrong? What will I do when the worst happens?*

Stanford University psychologist and author of *The Upside of Stress*, Kelly McGonigal, talks about the impact stress has on our ability to handle difficult moments. "Stress leaves an imprint on your brain that prepares you to handle similar stress the next time you encounter it. Psychologists call the process of learning and growing from a difficult experience stress inoculation. Going through the experience gives your brain and body a stress vaccine."[6] That reasoning is exactly why fighter pilots, elite athletes, emergency responders, and others who are required to perform under stress go through repetitions and practice dealing with stress.

RED FLAG LEADERSHIP

To be ready for combat, we spend weeks and months preparing, practicing, and planning for contingencies we might face on a deployment. We often train in worst-case scenario environments so we can be ready for anything. Even if the current conflict is a low-threat environment, we still train at the highest levels, preparing ourselves for the worst-case scenarios.

Red Flag is the Air Force's premier aerial combat training exercise. As described by the 414th Combat Training Squadron, the exercise provides aircrews the experience of multiple, intensive combat sorties in the safety of a training environment. The first Red Flag exercise occurred in 1975 to help the Air Force "train as it fights." Lessons from Vietnam showed that if a pilot could survive his first ten combat missions, then his probability of survival for the remaining missions increased substantially. Red Flag was designed to expose each pilot to their first ten combat missions in a training environment, enabling pilots to be more confident and effective in actual combat. Most deployed aircraft and personnel are part of the "blue force" that uses a variety of tactics to attack targets such as airfields, missile sites, and tanks. The enemy "red force" uses simulated anti-aircraft artillery, surface-to-air missiles, and electronic jamming equipment to defend the targets. In addition, red force aggressor pilots closely emulate known enemy aircraft and tactics. The goal of Red Flag is to prepare pilots, aircrew, and operators to fight against a peer-level adversary in any combat environment.

I was excited to go to Red Flag, but it was nerve-wracking, too. Once again, I wanted to prove myself. When we were not flying in the mission, we were watching and evaluating what other pilots did so there was plenty of room for feedback and criticism. If we did something stupid, we would certainly hear about it from our fellow pilots. The pressure to perform is high. As part of the Red Flag exercise, each unit is responsible for leading the mission during one of the execution scenarios.

Our unit is tasked to lead the air interdiction mission and I am selected to upgrade to mission commander, responsible for leading the entire mission package into war. Our mission is to attack targets deep in enemy territory, to destroy the enemy's military potential before it can be brought to bear effectively against friendly forces. We are also told to prepare for a combat search and rescue mission, meaning one of our pilots will likely be "shot down," and we will have to orchestrate the rescue to retrieve the pilot. As the mission commander, I will brief the mission, lead the execution of the mission, and then debrief the mission . . . talk about pressure.

I get the lowdown on assets, threats, and intent for the mission. Along with my package leads, I spend the day planning, seven hours of working with all units to coordinate the best plan of action to achieve the mission objectives and bring everyone home safely. In our planning process, we first prepare by gathering information: What is our mission? How will environmental factors affect the mission? What are the threats to the mission? What effects do we want to achieve? What capabilities do we have available? We then develop our plan by making sure every team lead understands each phase of the plan and clarify roles and responsibilities. During the planning process, we also take time to war game or do a walkthrough of our plan to help visualize our roles and ask questions along the way. Finally, we plan for contingencies by asking what-if questions. By planning for the most likely contingencies we might face, we can mitigate risk. We also have a red team go through our plan and ask tough questions so we can discuss what we will do if that contingency occurs. Red teams can challenge operational concepts to discover weaknesses before an adversary might. They can also serve as a devil's advocate, offering alternative interpretations and challenging established thinking. We prepare, practice, and plan for contingencies so we are ready to face the challenges in mission execution.

The day of execution is nerve-wracking, but I feel ready to go because of the intensive preparation and planning. I want it to go well, and I know everyone is counting on me for my leadership and decision-making. Of course, nothing ever goes as planned on a Red Flag mission, and there will be several real-time decisions to make. My first decision comes when several critical assets are late for the start of the exercise based on maintenance issues. I direct a "Rolex" (an adjustment to our timeline) to delay long enough to ensure we have all the required assets in place. The mission is still a go.

I lead our four-ship of A-10s across the push line, now crossing into what is considered enemy territory. We drop down low to 100 feet above the ground to avoid enemy radar. We are using a technique called terrain masking to hide behind the terrain and avoid being detected by enemy ground threats. We also hope to be safe in ground clutter and avoid detection from the enemy aggressor aircraft. We make our way into the target area undetected, and then pop up above the ridgeline to deliver our rockets and bombs on the enemy compound. As we maneuver to get out of the area, my radar warning receiver starts blaring, indicating an enemy missile is tracking my aircraft. I pull hard on the stick to get away from the threat while simultaneously dispensing chaff and flares. I dive back down to 100 feet to hide behind the terrain once again. My wingmen follow behind me working hard to escape the enemy threat. We make it out successfully, but not all friendly aircraft are so lucky on the mission. We get word that one friendly aircraft is shot down and there is an active combat search and rescue going on (all simulated, of course). We planned for this contingency, and everyone does their part to ensure the pilot is picked up successfully without further losses. And all of this is executed during one training mission. It is high stress, but by design. If we can achieve success in training, we are all better prepared for combat.

CONSIDERATIONS FOR LEADERS

As a fighter pilot, I've flown thousands of hours in a fighter jet with more than 100 missions in combat. The only certainty in all these missions . . . nothing ever goes exactly as planned. Just when we think we have a solid course of action, something happens that requires us to adjust and make changes. And if we're leading the formation, then we must be flexible and ready to change our plan as required to lead our wingmen to mission success.

We must evolve and adapt so that when the situation demands it, we are prepared to execute. So, how can we best prepare, practice, and plan for contingencies in our organizations?

Prepare: Do the work to be prepared.

- What research can be done in advance?
- What data or information are available to show what has (or hasn't) worked in the past?
- What are the objectives?

Practice: Practice, rehearse, or visualize to find opportunities for improvement. Practice creates clarity and boosts confidence among our team. Practice also improves buy-in when we include team members. Teams that have put in the work to practice will be more productive and are more likely to achieve success.

- Rehearse critical meetings and presentations.
- Meet with team members to do a walkthrough of new plans or decisions and assess how it might affect the organization.
- Clarify new roles and responsibilities.

Plan for contingencies: Planning for contingencies helps mitigate risk. Once we think through contingencies, we will be better prepared to execute, respond under stress, and face difficult moments.

- Where could things go wrong with the plan? What is the plan if things go wrong?
- What is the response to the worst-case scenario? Consider creating a red team to ask tough questions and review the plan from a different perspective.

In today's complex, dynamic environment, preparation is fundamental to success in leadership. Whether we are facing a difficult decision, making changes in our organization, or anticipating a critical meeting, we should prepare, practice, and plan for contingencies. *If you want to lead with courage, then do the work. Be prepared to respond and adjust when the mission (or life) doesn't go as planned.*

Chapter 5

WIGGLE YOUR FINGERS AND TOES

"The most difficult thing is the decision to act. The rest is merely tenacity. The fears are paper tigers. You can do anything you decide to do. You can act to change and control your life and the procedure. The process is its own reward."

—Amelia Earhart

Figure 5.1 After landing in Afghanistan from my first combat mission with Lieutenant Colonel Mike "Spanky" O'Dowd.

THE GLOBAL WAR ON TERRORISM

When the Global War on Terrorism began in late 2001, we were ready to go to war and do our part. Once President George W. Bush announced that al Qaeda was responsible for the 9/11 attacks and they had terrorist training camps in Afghanistan, we all wanted to get in the fight and eliminate the terrorists who had attacked our homeland. Like many Americans, we were enraged that the terrorists had attacked us on our own soil, killing thousands of innocent men, women, and children. We wanted to ensure it never happened again.

During this time, however, Air Force fighter squadrons, including A-10s from the 23rd Fighter Group, were still tasked to support no-fly zone operations in Iraq. Even though we were ready and willing to go to Afghanistan, our primary mission was still in Iraq. I had only been in the squadron for a few months when the 75th Fighter Squadron was tasked to deploy to Al Jaber Air Base in Kuwait to support Operation Southern

Watch. Our mission in the A-10 was to provide combat search and rescue (CSAR) if the Iraqis shot down one of our coalition aircraft. The CSAR mission involved aircraft and pilots specifically trained to find isolated personnel, coordinate rescue actions, escort helicopters, and suppress enemy forces while rescuing isolated personnel. CSAR is a mission A-10 pilots specifically train for, and it requires an upgrade to be a CSAR-qualified pilot, also known as a Sandy pilot (a call sign that goes back to fixed-wing search and rescue missions flown during the Vietnam War).

As coalition aircraft flew into Iraq to patrol the no-fly zone, A-10s were launched to be close by and ready to go if a coalition aircraft was shot down. We would accompany a mission package of aircraft whose primary role was to shoot down any Iraqi military aircraft in the exclusion area. Coalition aircraft were also authorized to defend themselves if fired on by enemy ground forces, surface-to-air missiles, or anti-aircraft artillery sites.

As a young wingman and new to the squadron, I was always number four in a four-ship formation of A-10s. My role as number four on a CSAR mission was to monitor the radio, support number three in escorting the rescue helicopters, and ensure nobody ran out of gas. We never wanted to be needed for CSAR, but we would be ready if the time came. For A-10 pilots, most Operation Southern Watch missions were spent listening on the radios and flying racetrack patterns in the sky over southern Iraq, then returning to Kuwait once the mission was complete. For pilots trained to engage the enemy, it was not particularly exciting, but it was still a much-needed mission for our brothers and sisters in arms.

As operations intensified in Afghanistan in early 2002, senior military leaders decided to move A-10s forward from Kuwait to Bagram Air Base in Afghanistan. Each A-10 squadron would first deploy to Kuwait to support Operation Southern Watch, then airplanes and pilots would rotate through Afghanistan during their deployment so we could support operations in both locations. It was not easy to support these two completely different missions, but everyone wanted to join the fight in Afghanistan, and this was our way to get there. The operations were remarkably different in each location; everything from munitions to maps had to be changed when moving from one location to another. In Iraq, we needed weapons capable of destroying hard targets such as tanks and artillery, but in Afghanistan, we needed weapons designed for soft targets such as mud buildings, vehicles, and troops in the open. Perhaps most critical, the rules of engagement were vastly different in each location, so we had to be on our game to remember how the rules differed. In Iraq, all the rules were based on self-defense; we could not attack anything or anyone unless they attacked us first. In Afghanistan, we worked with ground troops who gave us targets to strike if they met specific enemy criteria.

After a few weeks on the ground in Kuwait, our squadron started moving pilots and airplanes into Afghanistan to support Operation Enduring Freedom. I was eager to go because it appeared more relevant than what we were doing in Kuwait. Even though CSAR was a critical mission, the reality was we weren't doing much in Iraq. After 9/11, we were all ready to take the fight to the enemy. We wanted to go after the enemy that had attacked our homeland and killed thousands of innocent people. We also wanted to make a difference in supporting our troops on the ground to help them get home safely to their families. Close air support was our bread and butter, and we wanted in on the mission in Afghanistan.

PRESSURE TO PERFORM

One morning after breakfast, I got word I would be part of the next two-ship of airplanes to go into Afghanistan. We would be flying from Kuwait to Bagram Air Base in Afghanistan. This would officially be my first combat mission once arriving in Afghanistan. My flight lead was Lieutenant Colonel Mike "Spanky" O'Dowd. He was one of the more experienced pilots and I felt confident flying with him. He was a combat-tested pilot from Desert Storm, kind at heart, and a man of faith. He genuinely cared about us and looked after us pilots as if we were his own kids. He was the epitome of a calm and collected pilot. We packed our bags and prepared for the journey ahead.

By now, we had a solid plan of how to move aircraft from Kuwait to Afghanistan, but it would still require the support of other assets. Our air planners ensured we had tanker support along the way so we could refuel in flight. It would take several air refuelings to make our way to Afghanistan, fly a combat mission, and then land at Bagram Air Base. There was an entire team from Air Combat Command's Air Operations Squadron who planned our flight to ensure we had tanker support and diplomatic clearances to cross each country along the way.

We took off from Kuwait in the morning and made our way along the Persian Gulf, avoiding Iran, taking the long route to Afghanistan. As we crossed into the Gulf and looked into Iran, our radar warning receivers started singing. The small display in the front of our cockpit warned us of potential threats in the area. We could see, based on the display, that the Iranians were turning on their radars and looking at us with their acquisition radars. They could see us, but they were not locking onto us or tracking us. In response, our radar warning receivers started chirping at us to let us know the Iranian missile operators were watching us. It was eerie to think about what those missiles could do, but we just pressed ahead and ensured we stayed over international waters.

We had several air refuelings along the way before entering Pakistan. It wasn't my favorite part of flying, but a necessity if we were going to make it to Afghanistan without stopping. I had experience refueling during training back home, but this was different. If I couldn't connect my airplane with the boom of the tanker successfully, we would have to land at a nearby base owned by one of our allies. There weren't many good options, and it would be extremely embarrassing. It was a clear blue-sky day so we could easily see the tanker as it pulled out in front of us as we traversed the Persian Gulf. My flight lead hooked up first, making it look easy, and then it was my turn.

"Mazda 2, cleared to precontact," the boom operator announced over the radio.

I reduced my power slightly to drop below the tanker and then slowly pushed my power back up to position my aircraft 50 feet directly behind the boom of the tanker.

"Mazda 2, precontact, stabilized, and ready," I said as confidently as I could on the radio. I was doing my best to control my breathing and relax my death grip on the stick when I heard my flight lead calmly say, "wiggle your fingers and toes," a technique many pilots use to help relax during air refueling. He was clearly aware of the stress I was feeling.

We had perfect conditions that day, but it wouldn't always be like this; clouds and nighttime could make this 250-mph rendezvous in the sky exceedingly dangerous. The boom operator came over the radio and said, "Mazda 2, cleared to contact."

I slowly moved closer to the tanker, and eventually stabilized in the contact position. I was doing my best to be as smooth and stable as possible as the boom operator slowly moved the boom into position. I heard the clunk of the boom connecting with my airplane and a tug as I was now essentially being towed by the tanker.

"Contact," the boom operator said over the radio.

"Contact," I responded.

I breathed a small sigh of relief but remained focused on the director lights to stay in position. Director lights are two rows of lights on the underside of the tanker that help us fly in the ideal position; one lets us know whether to go up or down, the other forward or aft. Despite being connected to the tanker, I still had to remain stable long enough to fill up both the internal and external tanks we were carrying. After about five minutes of holding position, the boom operator told me I was topped off, so I hit the disconnect button on the stick, releasing my jet from the tanker's boom. I would have to repeat this procedure two more times before we could make our way successfully into Afghanistan, but the first test of my combat mission was a success.

That experience has stayed with me and been a reminder for me during challenging situations throughout my career where I felt pressure to perform. During these difficult moments when we're feeling stressed, instead of critiquing ourselves and worrying about what others will think, we should remember that those feelings of stress and fear are a normal response. Instead of looking at this stress as a negative reaction or a weakness, Stanford University psychologist and author of *The Upside of Stress*, Kelly McGonigal, describes how we should interpret stress: "1) view your body's stress response as helpful, not debilitating; 2) view yourself as able to handle, and even learn and grow from, the stress in your life; and 3) view stress as something that everyone deals with." She goes on to say that "once you appreciate that going through stress makes you better at it, it can be easier to face each new challenge."[1] We can all face stress and fear in many situations in our everyday lives; it's what we do in those moments that truly matters the most.

READY FOR COMBAT

As we crossed the border from Pakistan to Afghanistan, my senses heightened, and my adrenaline was pumping. I could not help but think back to 9/11. I wanted to do my part to ensure that an event like 9/11 never happened again. We would do everything we could to keep more Americans out of harm's way. The reality of taking lives was now more at the forefront of my mind. Could I do it? For me, the short answer was yes. My mission was about protecting our troops on the ground and that would mean I might have to kill the enemy to protect our troops. The enemy was certainly interested in taking us out, so for me, it was about defending our friendly troops and keeping Americans safe at home.

It turns out, my first combat mission was completely uneventful. We were tasked to support a ground unit, but no weapons were required, and we acted as an armed escort for a ground convoy. We didn't drop a single bomb, but we supported our brothers and sisters on the ground, none-theless. I quickly learned that just by being overhead, we helped ground troops be more confident as they patrolled small villages and traversed difficult terrain. We did our best to reassure them, to let them know we were ready if anything happened; we were the calm in the chaos for them, a reassuring voice overhead that told them we wouldn't let them down.

After an eight-hour mission, we finally began our approach to Bagram Air Base. Since there were unknown threats in the area, we started our approach high overhead the field, then spiraled down in what we called the whirlpool to end up at a low altitude over the runway. When we called for clearance to land, the tower controller told us we could only use one side of the runway. That was non-standard, but we followed the instruc-tions. As I began my final approach, I lined my A-10 up on the right side of the runway as directed before touching down. Once my wheels hit the ground, it immediately became clear why that restriction existed. The left side of the runway was riddled with potholes, and I occasionally saw rocks the size of golf balls littering the runway. I suddenly felt trapped on this now very narrow runway, knowing that if I veered off the wrong way, I would likely end up blowing a tire, and if I veered off the other way, I would end up off the prepared surface and into an area known to contain landmines. Neither option was a good one, so I focused intently on keep-ing my wheels on the runway while I taxied to park.

As I pulled into my parking spot, I looked out my cockpit to see smiling faces of pilots and maintenance troops in my squadron welcoming us to Afghanistan. I climbed down the ladder, achy from the long flight, and suddenly felt freezing water drenching me all over. Apparently, it was tra-dition (or had now become a tradition) to douse a pilot down with water to celebrate the milestone of a first combat mission. I was excited to be there with them, to finally be doing what I had been trained to do.

Life at Bagram often reminded me of my time as a cadet living in Jacks Valley during basic training. We only had one large tent for A-10 pilots and maintenance troops. The tent was always dusty since we left the flaps open to keep any breeze moving through. Not doing so would be detrimental to the health and well-being of all inside since showers and hygiene were hard to come by. I was the only woman deployed with our unit, but we all stayed in the same tent. There wasn't anywhere else to go, and I wanted to be with my squadron. I used my military-issued poncho to make my own little corner in the tent with a few more ponchos I borrowed from other pilots. I had my own space (six inches surrounding a cot) for sleep and some privacy, but I was still part of the team.

We flew and slept, but there was not much more to do. Living conditions were austere. We ate MREs (meals ready to eat) and took "showers" with baby wipes. After a few weeks, our engineers set up a shower building with a bucket of water and a shower sprayer that looked more like the sprayer you might find in your kitchen sink. This was all set up in an old bombed-out building so feeling clean afterward was relative. We made the most of our situation and spent a lot of time hanging out together in our downtime. We explored the base and checked out the remnants of old Soviet aircraft left there. We also pilfered any scrap wood we could find to turn one of the rooms in the base of the Afghan control tower into a movie room. It was not much, but we made it work. We had folding chairs and a TV with an assortment of DVDs. We made theater seating in the small room and decorated it with anything we could find at the local Afghan bazaar. Brightly colored rugs covered the floors and blocked the windows from light. It certainly helped us relax and recharge after coming back from long, often stressful missions.

Afghanistan was an interesting place to be in 2002. We had already made significant strides in rooting out the terrorists and eliminating their training camps by late 2001. We were all hoping to take the fight to the enemy, but, by summer 2002, there was little resistance, and we spent the majority of our time providing overwatch and convoy escort for our troops on the ground. For us, it could be eerily quiet as enemy forces regrouped and relocated to Pakistan. We could fly for hours on end only to come back and report NSTR—nothing significant to report. Even General Tommy Franks, the Commander of United States Central Command, stated, "It has been said that those who expect another Desert Storm will wonder every day what it is that this war is all about. This is a different war."[2] We did what we could to support the overall strategy of hunting down key individuals and learning more about al Qaeda's structure and plans for future operations. For A-10 pilots, that meant we spent our time

Figure 5.2 With my fellow Air Force Academy Class of 1997 class-mates (Pipes, Ox, Lindy, and Dozer) on our first deployment to Afghanistan.

providing overwatch for small teams of soldiers moving through villages in Afghanistan. We would stay overhead to be available to provide them support if needed. Yes, some missions felt more meaningful than others, but I soon realized how comforting it was for ground troops to simply have us overhead.

WE GOT YOU COVERED

On my second deployment to Afghanistan in 2005, the use of improvised explosive devices (IEDs) was on the rise in Afghanistan, so we spent a lot of time flying overhead convoys as they proceeded from one location to another throughout Afghanistan. Once an IED detonated, it was often met with an ambush on the remaining vehicles that stayed to help the stricken vehicle. To help prevent that potentially deadly situation, we would fly overhead and ahead of the convoy to look at the route they were taking. Did anything look out of the ordinary? We used to call these missions the search for "disturbed dirt." We would set up points along the route for one aircraft to look at through our targeting pods while the other aircraft flew overhead and looked at the bigger picture. I don't know if we ever really found anything looking at the dirt roads along the way, but just by being there we potentially thwarted enemy attacks and gave our forces confidence as they traversed treacherous terrain.

On one mission, we took off from Bagram Air Base with four different sets of coordinates to scan before a convoy arrived. We arrived in a remote area near the border of Pakistan and began to look at the coordinates through our targeting pod to see what was there. We had the coordinates in our system, so we could easily cycle between the points looking for threats before the convoy arrived. I went first with my wingman overhead looking out his cockpit for the big picture view while I stared through the soda straw of my targeting pod. We didn't see anything, and after about 15 minutes began to grow tired of staring at the dirt and waiting for the convoy. It didn't seem like we were doing anything worthwhile. Finally, the radio crackled, and we heard the voice of one of the convoy members:

> "We're making our way through the valley now. We don't have a qualified controller with us, and we have intelligence reports about a possible ambush."

I could hear the fear in his voice as he asked about the route ahead. Because they didn't have a qualified joint terminal attack controller, it would be more difficult to call in an airstrike because they didn't have the training required. If needed, this would be considered emergency close air support. It could be dangerous and required a methodical response to help ensure the safety of our forces.

"We got you covered," I said as calmly as I could over the radio. I relayed to the radio operator that we had been scanning the area for 15 minutes and could not see any threats in the area and we would stay with them until they arrived at their next FOB (forward operating base). I could almost sense his relief when I told him we would be there for the duration of his mission. We looked at the route as well as the hillsides along the route. We stayed with that convoy until they closed in on their FOB and reassured them along the way. We made sure they were safe.

That mission changed my view about convoy escort and support to our ground forces. We were often frustrated with convoy escort because, in our simplistic view, we were just flying circles overhead for hours on end. However, if it meant we deterred an attack just by being there or reassured a team on the ground, then it was worth it. It was all part of supporting our troops on the ground and helping them feel reassured while they conducted their missions.

SLOWER IS FASTER

An engine fire in an aircraft can be deadly. It's one of those critical emergencies in an A-10 when we have a boldface procedure, a critical emergency procedure presented in **BOLDFACE** capital letters. Pilots must be able to immediately accomplish these procedures in the published sequence without reference to the checklist. We practiced the engine fire checklist every time we were in the simulator during our emergency procedures training to make sure we could get it right under the stress of an emergency.

1. **THROTTLE/APU—OFF**
2. **FIRE HANDLE—PULL**
3. **AGENT—DISCHARGE**

A few weeks into my A-10 training, I was scheduled for my very first emergency procedures simulator. At this point, I was still dealing with my own helmet fire of trying to manage all the information in front of me. Since this was my first emergency procedures simulator, the instructor told me each emergency he would give me before it happened. So, I knew the engine fire boldface was coming, but it was still nerve-wracking. In the simulation, I was flying the airplane on a clear blue-sky day at about 10,000 feet above the ground. No significant weather. No dangerous terrain. Nothing else to complicate the mission. And then it happened.

My engine fire light illuminated at about the same time my simulated wingman called over the radio, "Hog 2, you have smoke coming out of your right engine."

The situation was clear. I had an engine fire light and confirmed smoke coming from the engine. I needed to execute the boldface for an engine fire. **THROTTLE – OFF**. I didn't hesitate. I quickly pulled the left throttle back and shut down the left engine. **FIRE HANDLE – PULL**. As I reached up to pull the fire handle (the next step in the boldface procedure), I immediately realized my mistake. I had shut down the good engine, the left engine. It was the right engine that was on fire. I just complicated the emergency.

The instructor hit the pause button on the simulator:

"Take a deep breath and try it again. New day. New jet."

Thankfully, we were in the simulator, and this wasn't a real mission. I took a few deep breaths to calm my nerves, then went through the boldface again, this time shutting down the correct engine to put out the fire. It was embarrassing, to say the least, but a good lesson to learn so early in my A-10 training.

Sometimes when we're faced with an emergency or a chaotic situation, we immediately feel like we need to act. It's often best to slow down and take a deep breath *before* we take the proper action. Moving too quickly and taking the wrong action can compound the problem, making the situation worse than it was, as was the case of shutting down the wrong engine. Instead of extinguishing the fire by shutting down the correct engine, my incorrect action resulted in one engine still on fire and one engine not operating. Not a good situation for an airplane with only two engines.

Just as we learned in pilot training, we need to follow a logical process to help us respond in an emergency or demanding situation. Maintain aircraft control. Analyze the situation. Take the proper action. Land as soon as conditions permit. If I had taken the time to clearly analyze the situation and confirm I was taking the proper action, I wouldn't have made the emergency worse.

"Sometimes slower is faster," my instructor coolly said. "Take a second to confirm you have the correct engine before shutting an engine down."

"Got it," I declared. I would not make the same mistake again.

I've had to deal with many stressful situations in the A-10, whether it was an aircraft emergency or a situation on the ground with friendly troops screaming for close air support. Each time, I remembered this lesson: take a deep breath. Sometimes acting too quickly can make the situation worse. When our brothers and sisters on the ground are requesting for us to get in there as quickly as possible, there is pressure to execute. But the consequences of acting too quickly without taking the time to analyze the situation can be deadly. How close are the friendly troops to the target? Can we clearly identify their location to ensure we don't cause fratricide? Take a deep breath, analyze the situation, and take the proper action.

As I progressed throughout my career, I carried this same lesson with me into my role as a commander and leader of teams. If I started to feel overwhelmed, angry, or frustrated in a situation, then I reminded myself to take a deep breath and take some time to think through the situation. Sometimes in the chaos, our best immediate reaction as a leader is to do nothing. Not every situation requires an immediate reaction. Most of the time we can stop, breathe, and take the time to think about how we will respond.

CALM IN THE CHAOS

Deploying to combat multiple times as a young fighter pilot demonstrated to me the significant role leaders play in remaining calm in chaotic situations. I watched many of my leaders set the example in both Afghanistan and Iraq with their ability to remain calm under pressure. They were always cool and collected on the radio, even when friendly ground troops were screaming for close air support. They recognized how important it was for them to be calm in the chaos to reassure our ground troops in some of the most chaotic and stressful situations. They also did their best to reassure us on the ground.

One of the most memorable examples occurred during the early days of Operation Iraqi Freedom. When the war kicked off in Iraq, we were required to wear varying levels of MOPP gear depending on the threat level. MOPP stands for mission-oriented protective posture, which is protective gear designed for use in a toxic environment, such as a chemical, biological, radiological, or nuclear strike. I will never forget the first alarm red we heard, an indication of an incoming missile. We were in our mission-planning cell getting ready for a mission when the alarm sounded. At the same time, an intelligence officer in the room next door yelled out to everyone, "Missile inbound! Missile inbound!"

We dropped everything and donned our remaining MOPP gear. We were already wearing our boots and overalls, so we only had to add our protective coats, mask, and gloves. We are trained to be able to put MOPP gear on as quickly as possible and then do buddy checks to make sure we got it right. I distinctly remember our director of operations calmly walking around the room, patting each of us on the head to let us know we were good, but also looking us directly in the eyes with calm reassurance to let us know we were going to be okay. It was a stressful few minutes waiting for the missile to impact, but the missile either missed or was destroyed by our air defense systems. Thankfully, there were no injuries or damages to the base this time. As scared as we all were in the moment, the small nod of assurance from my director of operations made all the difference. He remained calm, and he kept us all calm in the chaos.

Although the combat environment presents unique circumstances, leaders at all levels in any organization can serve their team well by remaining calm during a crisis. Teams want leaders who are consistent and remain calm and composed even under stress. Consistency creates trust. Our team wants to know they can count on us during tough times. It's still okay to admit we're stressed or scared in these difficult moments, but we also need to have a plan to deal with the stress and face the fear. We need to show our team we can remain calm, be decisive, and act even in the face of fear. Our team will be watching to see how we respond.

CONSIDERATIONS FOR LEADERS

Leaders play a pivotal role in demonstrating that we understand the intensity of a situation while also helping the team remain calm and composed under pressure.

- Prioritize clear, concise, and correct communication, especially during a crisis when people are eager for information. Tell them what you know and be honest about the situation.
- Instill confidence. Reassure the team that they are well prepared to endure hard times, even when the outcome remains uncertain.
- Empathize with team member stress levels and act/adjust accordingly.

To help our team develop and grow, we should teach them our techniques for overcoming stress and facing fear. Sometimes it's as simple as taking a deep breath or wiggling our fingers and toes. *If you want to lead with courage, then be calm in the chaos. Your team is watching to see how you will respond.*

Chapter 6

EMPOWER YOUR WINGMEN

"You gain strength, courage and confidence by every experience in which you really stop to look fear in the face. You are able to say to yourself, 'I have lived through this horror. I can take the next thing that comes along.' You must do the thing you think you cannot do."
—Eleanor Roosevelt

Figure 6.1 75th Expeditionary Fighter Squadron, Al Jaber Air Base, Kuwait, during Operation Iraqi Freedom.

ON THE PRECIPICE OF WAR

After coming home from our first deployment to Afghanistan at the end of 2002, we began to hear more on the news about a pending situation in Iraq. President Bush argued that the vulnerability of the United States following the attack on September 11, 2001, combined with Iraq's alleged possession and manufacture of weapons of mass destruction and its support to terrorist groups, made disarming Iraq a renewed priority. UN Security Council Resolution 1441 passed on November 8, 2002, demanding that Iraq readmit inspectors and that it comply with all previous resolutions.[1] It was clear the Bush administration was making the case to go to war.

As tensions mounted, we started preparing for another deployment to the Middle East. Our squadron was not tasked with anything yet, but we were making sure we would be ready if needed. Nobody wants war, but if there is a war, then we want to be part of it to go out and do what we have been trained to do. I equate it to playing on a sports team. You don't want to just practice, you want to play the game. You don't want to sit on the sidelines and watch when you've been practicing and preparing; you want to play in the game so you can make an impact. I felt the same way about going to combat. If my team was going, then I wanted to be with them.

The 75th Fighter Squadron was given a prepare-to-deploy order in early February 2003. We knew we were prepared and our presence as A-10 pilots could help save lives on the ground.

Crossing the pond (otherwise known as the Atlantic Ocean) was no small task. Again, we had an entire team of people who planned our flight to ensure we had tanker support and diplomatic clearances to cross each country along the way. The plan was to take off before sunrise and spend the day flying across the Atlantic, eventually making our way to Lajes Field on Terceira Island in the Azores. It was my first trip across the pond in an A-10 and I was excited, but nervous as well. It's a long stretch of ocean and if things went wrong, there weren't many options. In addition to all our normal flight gear, we had to wear what we refer to as a "poopy suit," officially called an anti-exposure watertight suit, which would be critical for survival if we had to eject into the ocean. As if we weren't already uncomfortable enough, this was downright miserable to wear. It was tight and constricting from our neck to our toes but would keep us alive if we had to eject.

In addition to the discomfort of wearing a poopy suit, we dealt with terrible weather, flying for hours in the clouds in close formation, tied to the tanker so we wouldn't lose them and then be unable to get gas. It could be a stressful seven hours when the weather conditions were poor. And when the weather was good, well, it could be utterly boring, trying to pass the time and find ways to stay awake after the early morning takeoff. But the reward was landing in the Azores, feeling the fresh ocean breeze, ditching all the uncomfortable flight gear, and finally making it to a real bathroom. After a quick shower, we would head to town to Pescadores, a pilot favorite, to order Swordfish Cataplana with plenty of drinks to go around. We would have an entire day of rest on the island so we could relax before the next flight, which would be even longer than the first.

OPERATION IRAQI FREEDOM, 2003

We finally arrived at Al Jaber Air Base in Kuwait on March 1, 2003. As we landed and taxied in, I was shocked and amazed at the number of aircraft lining the ramps. I had been to Al Jaber Air Base a year prior in support of

Operation Southern Watch, and this display was nothing like I had seen before. A-10s, F-16s, F/A-18s, and rescue helicopters lined the parking ramp as far as you could see. It was clear we were prepared and ready to go to war.

Despite the heavy buildup of aircraft, we sat for two weeks watching the news, getting intelligence briefings, and guessing about what might happen and when. We did not talk much about the politics of the war, we just focused on what our role would be. Our job was to execute orders, and that is where we dedicated our efforts. We focused on our mission. We knew our role in the A-10 community would be to support our troops on the ground. It is a straightforward role but can get complicated based on the threat level and disposition of friendly and enemy forces.

We spent our days studying threats, building maps for the squadron, and mission planning for different scenarios. At night, we would retreat to pilot town (a series of sleeping trailers in the center of base designated for pilots) and have near-beer (non-alcoholic beer) and smoke cigars. On a good night, Dos Gringos (a band formed by pilots) would sing songs about flying and fighting. It was a way to let loose and decompress after another day of waiting. As a wingman in the squadron with just over 300 hours in the A-10, I often wondered if I would be chosen to fly in combat missions or if I would just work in our mission-planning cell. Most of our experienced pilots had well over 1,000 hours in the airplane by this point. Still, I wanted to fly and be a part of the combat effort.

It turns out we would need every pilot we had with us to fill the sortie requirements we were tasked to fly. I would be flying missions, just like every other pilot in the squadron. A few weeks into the war, we would bring over even more pilots to help us fill the requirements. Our squadron would use combat pairs to ensure the least experienced members in the squadron, the wingmen, would be paired with more experienced pilots who were qualified as flight leads or instructors in the airplane. We would fly as the same combat pair for weeks at a time because it created efficiencies in our communication and tactics.

In our downtime, we had open and honest discussions with each other about the potential threats to our missions. We knew we might lose some airplanes and we may not bring everyone home. We were all a little scared (even if we didn't want to admit it) about what was to come. But we were also ready to face the challenges because we had prepared, we had practiced, and we had planned for contingencies. My squadron commander told us that to fly, we would all have to write letters home so if we did not make it, then he would have letters from us to give to our families. Talk about a reality check at 27 years old! I wrote letters to my parents, my husband, and my brother. Thankfully, none of them had to be delivered.

On March 17, President Bush declared an end to diplomacy and issued an ultimatum to Saddam Hussein, giving the Iraqi president 48 hours to leave Iraq. On March 19, we all gathered to listen to the president's address to the nation. We were ready. It was go time, and we all knew it. When Saddam Hussein refused to leave Iraq, US and allied forces launched an attack on the morning of March 20th. US aircraft dropped several precision-guided bombs on a bunker complex in which the Iraqi president was believed to be meeting with senior staff. Aircraft then followed with a series of airstrikes directed against government and military installations. Within days, US forces had invaded Iraq from Kuwait in the south.[2] Our mission in the A-10 community would be to support our ground troops as they made their way to Baghdad.

During our deployment, I received some advice from one of my mentors that I should write in a journal each day to record my thoughts. He was pushing me to spend some time reflecting on critical moments in my life. Although I was often too tired to write at the end of each day, I did spend time recording my views about each mission and what I was feeling and thinking. It also allowed me to decompress at the end of each day by putting my thoughts and often fears and frustrations down on paper. I found that by acknowledging my fears, I was better equipped to deal with them the next day.

20 MARCH 2003 (PERSONAL JOURNAL EXCERPT)

It's now 6:00 a.m. on the 20th of March in Kuwait. We spent most of the night taking a series of naps due to the continuous alarm reds [an alarm indicating that a missile attack was imminent or in progress] almost every hour. I don't know if the Iraqis realize how much they are pissing us off. Everyone here is ready for the air war to start so we can get business done.

The first alarm red was yesterday morning with an actual missile in the air on its way somewhere in Kuwait. It definitely makes your heart beat a little faster. It's even worse when you hear the sirens in the middle of the night. At least we're all getting pretty good at putting on the chem gear now.

We've been watching the news as much as possible when we're not busy mission planning. We all got together to watch the President's speech, so we're ready and we're fired up. It's really just a matter of time now waiting for the execute order. We know it's going to be soon.

I've finally finished writing letters to my family. Those have been the most difficult letters I've ever had to write. I just hope they never have to get them. We all try not to think of that as much as possible, but writing those letters makes you sit down and think about life after you're gone. Not something anyone wants to think about. After all, we're supposed to be invincible.

It's time to start a new day. Hopefully, this will be it.

On March 21st, the war officially kicked off. Our primary task was to support the Army as they made their way to Baghdad. As we held high overhead, monitoring the situation, we could see a line of dust as our friendly forces pushed their way into Iraq. It was an impressive sight. However, during the first week, there was little need for close air support and few targets for A-10s to destroy.

27 MARCH 2003 (PERSONAL JOURNAL EXCERPT)

It's 9:00 p.m. on Thursday. We were back in the air today. We took off with plans to go to Karbala, just south of Baghdad. Threats in the area, as long as we stayed out of the super MEZ [missile engagement zone], were Rolands [a short-range air defense missile system] and an SA-2 [a high-altitude air defense missile system] that had already fired guided missiles. Before we stepped, we talked about our plan if we got hit and had to eject. We would limp the jet back to friendlies south of Karbala by about 40 miles if we could make it. At least that was the plan.

Then we moved on to better topics like how we would plan our attacks, a much better subject. Anyhow, we took off, got gas, got passed to the GFAC [ground forward air controller], and then once again found no targets in the area where they had us look. We had to bingo out [depart for fuel] fairly quickly since we had to have enough gas to divert to PSAB [Prince Sultan Air Base in Saudi Arabia] since the weather was so bad at Jaber. We ended up getting gas again on the way home to make it back with enough fuel to divert. Even then, I had to get waived below my [weather] minimums to land. That was probably the worst part of the mission, the actual approach. I felt more stress during that landing than I did flying near Baghdad.

We could actually see the smoke over Baghdad from where we were, very strange. It's almost unreal to think about how far north into Iraq we've been flying. Lots of RWR [radar warning receiver] indications so far, but no missile launches or AAA [anti-aircraft artillery]. Either we're not seeing it or we're just lucky. I'll take it though!

30 MARCH 03 (PERSONAL JOURNAL EXCERPT)

It's been a few days since my last entry, so I'll try to catch up. I've been so tired the past few days that I couldn't keep my eyes open to write. I'm still exhausted, but it seems too early to sleep. It's now 6:30 pm on Sunday night. Let me backtrack a few days. I flew on the 28th on yet again another sortie without dropping bombs. We ended up doing more recce [reconnaissance] up near Baghdad. I did get a better look at the city; it was covered in dark black smoke from some of the trenches filled with oil that the Iraqis have set on fire. It's still amazing to me that we're almost there, it's hard to imagine what's next. I just wish we had been doing more on some of our sorties, but I know those guys need the recce done. We eventually find targets, but it all takes time, and we're all impatient.

After flying on the 28th, I ended up sitting alert yesterday. We sat Sandy [Combat Search and Rescue] alert for six hours and thankfully didn't get launched.

Now on to today . . . I got to fly twice. Our first sortie was uneventful. We had targets before we stepped but couldn't find anything in the target area. There were a few clouds so that didn't help either. At least we had a second sortie to make up for it. We had a few more pre-planned targets for the second sortie, but we ended up getting a task to a GFAC [ground forward air controller] instead. We went to Nasiriyah, just outside of Tallil where our guys were try-ing to take out the Fedayeen Saddam [an Iraqi paramilitary group that led guerrilla-style attacks on coalition forces]. We dropped our bombs on some enemy artillery pieces with good secondaries on my second set of bombs. The GFAC wanted us to save our guns and Mavs [Maverick missiles] to take out a building with the Fedayeen but we couldn't ID [identify] it as definitely military. They were hoping we would see guys out on the roof with AK-47s and mortar pits, but we couldn't see anything from the air [using only binocu-lars to help us identify targets]. I would have been happy to take them out since they were responsible for some of the brutal execu-tions and torture of our guys. Unfortunately, in the middle of a city, we can't take that risk.

2 APRIL 03 (PERSONAL JOURNAL EXCERPT)

What a day! I'm exhausted, but it's been a busy day, so I need to write it down before I forget. I ended up flying three sorties today with the 1st sortie going into Tallil, Iraq. It was pretty amazing to land in Iraq and then walk around the base, especially considering we were there not too long ago taking out targets. We were only there for about an hour, but we were able to take some photos in front of Saddam's pictures. In the ops [operations] building there, they have all the aircraft in the inventory listed with specific capa-bilities, including the A-10s. It's so strange to see that and know they've been studying us.

After Tallil, we flew to a kill box [a three-dimensional area used to identify a certain location on a map] just outside of Baghdad. It's definitely the closest to Baghdad that I've ever been. We were sent up there to kill 20–40 tanks, but they were nowhere to be found. We even had SEAD [suppression of enemy air defense] support and targeting pod assets. It's too bad they weren't there; it would have been great to remove those tanks from the battlefield.

We ended up going to the MEF [Marine Expeditionary Force] area to an open kill box and had a military compound as our dump target. We hit several enemy vehicles, some in revetments and some out in the open. I fired 640 rounds of the gun and dropped 4 MK-82s [500lb bombs]—it was a good day!

6 APRIL 03 (PERSONAL JOURNAL EXCERPT)

Well, today was a pretty good day. Bino [Lieutenant Colonel Rick Turner] and I flew up to Baghdad today and were immediately tasked to work with a GFAC who had a target area north of Baghdad city center. When we got to the target area, we realized it was an old SA-2 site in the traditional setting. We were looking for tanks, but all we found were tank tracks. Also, while we were checking out the site, I found two sets of missiles just staring up at us. We strafed both missile sites, but no secondaries—guessing they were decoys.

The GFAC also gave us clearance to take out the building next to the SAM [surface-to-air missile] site that was supposed to be an HQ building for a mech [mechanized] infantry division. We dropped 8 MK-82s on the buildings and got some amazing secondaries, missiles were cooking off everywhere, good thing we weren't too low.

After that, Bino put an EO (electro-optical) maverick into a bunker door below the SA-2 site and we watched it blow everything out the backside of the bunker. It was awesome. And then finally we both strafed 2 HETs [heavy equipment transporters] in the middle of an open field, one carrying a tank and the other with a launcher on the back. Not a bad day overall.

SEIZING THE MOMENT

By Monday, April 7, 2003, Operation Iraqi Freedom had been underway for almost three weeks.

Though coalition troops had reached Baghdad, the city is not yet under complete coalition control. On April 5th units from the Army's 3rd Infantry Division (ID) arrived in Baghdad to conduct a series of raids to probe, isolate, and destroy the last of the remaining Iraqi defenses subsequently popularized as the Thunder Run.[3] As part of the Thunder Run, April 7th would see some of the heaviest fighting when units from the 3rd ID conducted simultaneous offensives to capture the government center, the Green Zone, and secure all the major expressway intersections leading in and out of Baghdad.

The mission that day for our two-ship of A-10s (call sign Yard 05) is to fly to Baghdad, refuel in flight, and then hold for a tasking. The firefight is intense, and the situation on the ground is only getting worse, so there are dozens of aircraft stacked up all over Baghdad waiting to provide support and save lives.

I've relived this moment from April 7, 2003, many times over the last 20 years. Each time I talk about it or tell the story, I can see it, I can hear it, and I can feel it. And so I want you to relive it with me, too, to be here with me in the moment to feel my fear, but more importantly, to share in the lessons learned.

The radio interrupts the silence in my cockpit, "Yard 05, this is Advance 33. My guys are taking fire in the northern part of town. Grid is Mike Bravo 396 990. Rocket propelled grenade teams are working on the east side of the Tigris River putting RPGs into my guys." The hair on the back of my neck stands up, and my adrenaline is pumping. Lives are on the line.

The frantic calls we receive are coming from one of the units from the 3rd ID that had secured the main north–south expressway and the northernmost part of Baghdad. We listen carefully as the ground controller describes the situation on the ground. Our troops are on the west side of the Tigris River awaiting resupply, and small units of the Iraqi Republican Guard are on the east side of the river firing rocket-propelled grenades into our forces. Unfortunately, the weather conditions are terrible, and we can't see the ground below.

The ground controller gives us a target to strike that is underneath a prominent bridge in northern Baghdad. We pull out our maps to plot the target location as well as the friendly location, using a grease pencil to mark their positions on the map. We don't want to make a mistake that could jeopardize friendly forces.

Heading to the target, we stay above the weather until the very last second.

"Wedge—Shooters—Guns," my flight lead informs me of the formation and weapon for our attack and then confirms I am ready to go.

"One's ready."

"Two's ready."

We use our guns and rockets against the enemy location to help our
troops on the ground survive. I set up for my last rocket pass.

"Two's in from the south," I declare over the radio.

"Cleared hot, Two," comes the quick reply.

I fine-tune my aim point and press my thumb down on the weapons
release button, rippling seven rockets down on the enemy.

I pull off target to regain my altitude.

BOOM . . . I feel a large explosion at the back of my airplane. I see a
bright red-orange flash as the fireball envelopes my airplane. My heart
races and my adrenaline pumps. I am breathing rapidly against the pressure of my oxygen mask, and my mouth is going dry with the increase in
oxygen flow. I key the mic, "Two got hit. Two got hit."

The jet rolls left and points directly down at Baghdad below. It's not
responding to any of my control inputs. The ground is getting closer, and
I know I might have to eject. I quickly try to analyze the situation.

Master caution light.

Hydraulic lights.

Hydraulic gauges are at zero . . . the system has no pressure. It's empty.

I am plunging toward the ground completely out of control.

Ejection handles? No, not yet. The last thing I want to do is eject into
the hands of the enemy. I need to make every second count. I set aside
my fear, engage the backup emergency system, and regain control of the
airplane. I am flooded with relief as the jet starts responding to my inputs
and begins to climb up and away from Baghdad. For the first time, I think
I might make it out of here alive.

When my airplane was hit, and in the roughly 20 seconds that passed
(which felt like an eternity) I was aware of all the things that could go
wrong, and there were a lot of them. But despite all of this, I knew I had
to act. I had to do something if I was going to survive. All my attention was
on getting the jet under control. I didn't have time to open a checklist or
ask for help, I just had to react. Thankfully, my training kicked in and I
was able to respond.

Now that the jet is flying, my priority is to get out of Baghdad. I know if
I still have to eject, my chances of survival and rescue will be much better

outside the city. We start maneuvering south to get out of the city and anti-aircraft artillery begins coming up from everywhere. They are shooting at us again. Amazingly, we make it out of Baghdad and above the clouds with no further battle damage.

It turns out, a missile had hit the back of my airplane and metal from the explosion pierced the fuselage, creating hundreds of holes and damaging my flight control systems. The A-10 was built to take hits. It was built so if one hydraulic system is lost, the other will take over, and if both systems fail, there's still a backup system called manual reversion. Manual reversion is a backup to the backup system that allows the pilot to fly the aircraft under mechanical control. Cables and pulleys run from the control stick out to the control surfaces on the wings and tail of the aircraft. When hydraulics are removed from the aircraft (or in my case, dumped out in an explosion), the pilot can use cables and pulleys to fly the aircraft by moving small tabs on the control surfaces.

According to the Air Force Human Resources Lab, the inclusion of the manual reversion flight control system gives the A-10 an added margin for survival, but aircraft control in the manual flight mode is exceptionally demanding of piloting skills. As early as 1973, it was reported that there existed an "unacceptable pilot workload for the landing task in the manual reversion mode." As flight testing of the A-10 continued, it was found that "the most significant deficiencies noted were unacceptable load factor/pitch attitude excursions encountered during transition from the normal flight control systems to the manual system at high speed." The report also stated that "pilot-initiated transition to manual flight control mode and subsequent flight and landings could be accomplished, but not without an excessive pilot workload."[4]

I know I have a decision to make, stay with the jet and try to land or get to friendly territory and eject. The decision can be the difference between life and death, and it weighs heavily on me.

We didn't train very often in manual reversion. We only did it once during our initial training, so we knew how the jet would respond. The checklist for manual reversion landing was something we didn't practice at all. In the checklist, it said to attempt a manual reversion landing under ideal conditions only. *Ideal conditions? Ideal emergency? What does that even mean?* I know trying to land is a risk, but I also have many factors going my way. The jet is flying well, the winds are down the runway, and I have a very experienced flight lead with me providing vital support.

I have less than an hour to make this critical decision. I'm nervous to make the wrong decision. Part of me wants my flight lead to make the decision for me, to just tell me what to do. But he doesn't tell me what to do. Instead, he empowers me to make the decision. He says, "KC, you are flying a single-seat airplane, the decision is yours. I will back you up with whatever you decide." Even though I'm scared, I know I must act. I have to decide.

According to military records, ejection seats are about 90% effective today, but there are still risks of injuries. Because I weighed less than the ejection seat recommended, I had to sign a waiver saying I was aware of the potential for flailing injuries associated with the ejection seat. According to the Smithsonian, women pilots are especially at risk "because the lighter the object, the faster the toss and the greater the oscillation."[5] Ejecting from an aircraft moving at high speeds can be exceptionally dangerous. "The force of ejecting at those speeds can reach in excess of 20 Gs—one G is the force of Earth's gravity. At 20 Gs, a pilot experiences a force equal to 20 times his or her body weight, which can cause severe injury and even death."[6] In the event of an ejection, a catapult fires the ejection seat up the rails, a rocket then fires to propel the seat higher, and the parachute opens to allow for a safe landing. Pilots who have survived an ejection have described it as one of the most violent experiences of their lives.

After evaluating all the factors, I decide I am going to try to land the airplane. I feel confident in my training and preparation, and I am confident I can land the airplane successfully. Is there risk involved in my decision to land? Absolutely. We cannot operate without risk, but we must take calculated risks. We need to think through the consequences of the decisions we make. When we take risks, we need to fully understand what we are doing and the ramifications of our actions. I decided to land my airplane because I evaluated the situation and the risk involved, and I felt confident I could land the airplane successfully.

I am also keenly aware that A-10 pilots had attempted manual reversion landings only three times previously during Operation Desert Storm. Unfortunately, not all were successful. One pilot died when his jet crashed on landing. One aircraft was severely damaged after touching down only to discover he had no brakes or steering. The aircraft swerved on and off the runway several times; the pilot was lucky to survive. However, there was a glimmer of hope in that there was one successful manual reversion landing in an aircraft with similar damage to mine. I had heard these stories from talking to other A-10 pilots who shared their experiences with me. Although these pilots were not actually with me over Baghdad, their stories were. Their experiences, their sacrifice, I remembered it when I needed it most. They helped me survive, they helped me get home safely, and I am truly thankful for those stories. Sharing our experiences, good and bad, even when they expose mistakes or weaknesses, can help make other people better. And in some cases save their lives!

The flight back to base is one of the longest hours of my life. I don't know what will happen when I attempt to land. *Will I be able to control the airplane? Will I crash? Will I even survive?* I try to keep busy, but it's difficult. I have moments of thinking of the worst that could happen. I fear crashing; I am not ready to die. *I'm young. I still want to have kids.* My husband and I had been married about four years, but we had not spent a lot of time together due to deployments. I feel like we have so much life left to live together. Despite those thoughts occasionally creeping in, I know I have to focus on the task . . . just get home . . . just get to friendly territory. I pray and talk to God frequently on the way home. I pray I will survive. I pray I will land the airplane successfully. I pray I won't screw up. And I tell God in those moments that if He will just let me make it home, then I will tell the story and share my experiences as many times as people ask to help others and to teach others about my experience.

Flying back to base is both mentally and physically exhausting. I have heard pilots compare flying in manual reversion to driving a dump truck or a semi-truck without power steering. I have not done either, so I don't know if it is true, but I can tell you that it is exceedingly difficult to fly for an hour under those conditions. Just as the Air Force Human Resources Lab had promised, flying in manual reversion for that length of time is "exceptionally demanding of my piloting skills." Thankfully, pilots from Desert Storm had shared some of their manual reversion flying techniques with me. I take turns flying with my left hand on the stick, right hand on the stick, both hands on the stick so I am prepared to land normally (left hand on the throttle, right hand on the stick) when the time comes. Once again, those stories and techniques give me courage on my own challenging mission.

We finally cross into friendly territory and descend through the clouds to start the controllability check. I need to find out if I can even configure the airplane and make it all the way down to landing. I slow the aircraft, and it immediately becomes much harder to control. I am flying with both hands on the stick to maintain control. Then the pitch trim kicks in, and the aircraft levels out. [The purpose of pitch trim is to free the pilot from having to exert a constant pressure on the controls.] Eventually, my airplane becomes easier to control at a slower speed. Now we just need to make sure I can get the gear down with the emergency gear extension procedure.

Gear handle—down.

AUX landing gear extension handle—pull.

It feels like an eternity waiting for the three green lights, representing each wheel on my airplane. And then finally, all three lights illuminate, telling me the gear is down and locked.

Now, I just have to find the runway through the standard haze associated with the constant dust storms in Kuwait. We contact the tower controller and the supervisor of flying to let them know we are on our way in. The crash recovery team is waiting for me, and the rescue helicopters are on alert in case I have to eject. I don't want to use any of them, but it is reassuring to know there is an entire team waiting to support me, no matter the outcome. It is time to make my first radio call. Before this, my flight lead had made all the radio calls and done all the coordination. I am determined to sound calm and controlled on the radio. If I sound good, then I think I can convince everyone, including myself, that I am calm and controlled, and I can handle this. I practice a few times and then I make the call, "Yard 06, emergency, gear down, full stop."

I start down the final approach. Sixty feet to go.

I cross the landing threshold. The aircraft starts a quick roll to the left . . . my heart skips a beat. *Am I going to crash? Is my airplane going to flip over on its back? Do I even have time to eject?* I yank the stick back to the right and the aircraft levels out.

Thirty feet to go. *Please let me make it.*

Ten feet to go. Time stands still.

Almost there. *Just hold it steady.*

Main landing gear. Nose gear. *My jet is on the ground.*

The fire trucks are rolling toward me.

I take a deep breath. "Thank you, God."

I am relieved beyond imagination.

It turns out my landing is one of the best I have ever done; at least it sure feels that way. It is a huge relief to be back on the ground, but the best part is hearing the pilots in my squadron on the radio as I roll down the runway. Several had been standing by in their jets waiting to launch and they are watching and waiting for me to return. I will never forget the words of encouragement and support I heard from them that day.

"Beautiful."
"Way to go."
"Nicely done."
"Yeah, baby, good job!"
"Nicely done, KC."

The tower controller relays, "Yard 06, emergency response vehicles are on their way out. Let me know if we can do anything else for you."

My jet is now slowly rolling down the runway. I am so relieved and just thankful to be on the ground that I don't think much of bringing the jet to a complete stop. Finally, my flight lead radios from overhead, "Okay KC, you can bring it to a stop now."

I slowly apply the brakes knowing I will not have nose wheel steering and I will only have five brake attempts with the backup emergency system. The jet finally rolls to a stop.

Once I get the jet stopped with the emergency braking system, I am ready to get out of the jet and see the extent of the damage. The crash recovery crews meet me at the jet along with the wing commander. All are anxious to see the battle damage. I only have a description from my flight lead about what it looks like, so I am anxious to see the airplane as well. When I look at the back of the aircraft, I am shocked at the amount of damage. The airplane is riddled with holes. There is a large hole in the right horizontal stabilizer, the back tail section of the airplane. My right tail took a significant amount of shrapnel damage as well. Luckily, the jet was designed to take these hits. Although never confirmed, weapons experts believe that a surface-to-air missile impacted near the right horizontal stabilizer. Unfortunately, we never saw it coming.

Today, the A-10 has an upgraded countermeasures system. With the new system, the aircraft can sense an infrared missile, automatically dispense chaff and flare, and provide an audible warning to let the pilot know to maneuver the aircraft. That system would have been a lifesaver in Operations Desert Storm and Iraqi Freedom for many of the pilots who were hit without warning from surface-to-air missile systems.

The shrapnel that went into the fuselage sheared the left and right hydraulic lines in two separate locations. Although the right and left hydraulic lines are separated to provide additional survivability, much of the shrapnel went through the right side of the aircraft and then impacted the left interior side of the fuselage. The right pitch cable was also sheared, but due to aircraft design, there was no discernible effect on stick response.

The right engine also received shrapnel damage, but all engine indications were normal. I did not even know about this damage until after I landed, though my flight lead asked me several times on the way back what my engine indications were and if I was having any trouble with the right engine. If I had lost an engine, my situation would have been very different, and I likely would have been riding a parachute down into Baghdad.

The backside of the jet was charred and covered with hydraulic fluid. We are still not sure exactly what caused the fire or how long it lasted, but it caused no noticeable structural issues in flying the jet back. Considering the damage this jet took, it flew extremely well. It was a true testament to the durability of the A-10. I am incredibly thankful to those who designed, built, and maintained this airplane.

Figure 6.2 With Lieutenant Colonel Rick "Bino" Turner after landing on April 7, 2003. After landing, we realized just how much damage had been done to the airplane.

Photo credit: Alan Lessig, *Air Force Times.*

IT'S STILL ABOUT THE TEAM

It wasn't just my airplane that helped me get home successfully. My flight lead, Lieutenant Colonel Rick "Bino" Turner, was a critical asset in helping me make it back safely. We were truly a team that worked together in a highly stressful situation to overcome adversity. We trusted each other and had full confidence in each other's abilities. He provided me guidance and support when I needed it most. He empowered me to make a critical decision and supported me in that decision. The other members of my team, my maintenance crew chiefs, then Staff Sergeant Ian Morace and Senior Airman Randy Andrus, were back at our home base waiting for me to return. They were critical in preparing my airplane for this mission. We put an incredible amount of trust in our maintenance team, and in return, they do not want to let us down. They want us to succeed.

Figure 6.3 With my crew chiefs, Senior Airman Randy Andrus and Staff Sergeant Ian Morace after landing on April 7, 2003. Our maintenance teams did tremendous work during this deployment despite often unbearable working conditions.

I am thankful for their expertise and attention to detail in ensuring my jet could fly under any circumstances, even after extensive battle damage.

My crew chief was the first person I wanted to see after landing my airplane. Of course, I had to catch a ride back to my parking spot since my airplane needed to be towed off the runway. It was important to me to see my crew chief and apologize for bringing his jet back in that condition. As we pulled into the parking spot (in a car, not an airplane), he came over to me with the biggest smile, shook my hand, and said, "Ma'am, we're glad to have you back home."

We truly were a team that came together during a highly stressful combat mission. When you trust the members of your team, recognize their expertise, and empower them to make decisions, you create an environment where your team can excel.

TRUST AND EMPOWERMENT

That was a challenging mission for me, but it was also a defining moment in my life. That mission pushed me to my limits, but it also showed me what I was capable of. I got to see the impact of effective leadership on a team from the perspective of being at the lower levels of an organization. As a result of this mission, my leadership supported and encouraged new ideas, even from one of the youngest and least experienced members of the team. I saw firsthand what it was like to be a member of a high-performing team with a leader who could motivate and inspire a team during tough times. I saw what it was like to have a leader who empowered their team to make decisions and act.

During our time in Iraq, each flight lead was empowered to make their own decisions, act in critical moments, and execute the mission they were tasked to do. We didn't always know the situation we would face or what would be demanded of us, but we fully understood the rules of engagement and our commander's intent. Our leadership trusted us to do our job and to do it well. We didn't have to radio back and ask permission in the heat of battle. We were fully empowered to make time-critical decisions to execute the mission. At the same time, if something went wrong on a mission, then we would have to own it. But our leadership also supported us and had our back if we were operating within the commander's intent.

CONSIDERATIONS FOR LEADERS

It takes courage to empower a team and relinquish some control. To empower our wingmen or team members to make their own decisions successfully, we must take the following actions:

- Ensure our team members have the necessary training. Encourage teammates to be confident in their choices based on solid planning and preparation.
- Confirm team members understand the mission, vision, and intent.
- Seek ideas and input. Show team members that you trust their experience and value their expertise.
- Allow room for mistakes. Give team members the authority to solve their own problems.

Trusting and empowering our team can expedite the decision-making process and open more time for the leader to adjust their focus onto the bigger picture. *If you want to lead with courage, then trust your team and empower your wingmen.*

Chapter 7

THE FIGHTER PILOT DEBRIEF

"I have learned that success is to be measured not so much by the position that one has reached in life as by the obstacles which he has overcome while trying to succeed."

—Booker T. Washington

Figure 7.1 Debriefing our April 7, 2003 sortie with our maintenance team. I wish I could remember what I wrote in the maintenance log book . . . Code 3 Battle Damage—hydraulic systems inoperative, approximately 600 holes, needs sheet metal work?

OWNING ACCOUNTABILITY

Perfection is a goal, never a reality, in a fighter pilot's mind. We're always striving to improve, and a fighter pilot debrief allows us to do just that. In a debrief, we talk about our mission objectives. Did we meet them? Where did we succeed and where did we fail? We check our rank at the door so the more junior members can input freely and can provide feedback to the more senior members in the flight. We hold each other accountable. We don't take it personally because it's important that we all learn from each other's mistakes. By shifting our focus to identify suboptimal outcomes (not just talking about what we did well), to identify their causes, and to act on lessons learned, we drive cultural change within our organization. Cultural change ensures we evolve as a team, meet ever-evolving requirements, and can excel in a competitive environment.

THE COMBAT DEBRIEF

After we came in from the flight line on April 7, 2003, still riding high on adrenaline, we sat down to do what we do after every mission . . . an open and honest fighter pilot debrief. Even though I made it back successfully, we were not content to ride that success. We had to go back and look at what could be done better the next time. In addition to discussing the things we did wrong or could improve, we also talked about what went well. On this day, as one of the youngest and least experienced members of my deployed squadron, I was able to share my lessons learned, to talk about what I had done to be successful. My peers and superiors listened and thoughtfully evaluated what I had to say.

Debriefs are a powerful accountability tool for any team or organization. They enable us to fail forward, learning from our failures and mistakes and those of others without judgment. When we evaluate our performance, we create a culture of continuous improvement by holding each other accountable. The key here is that successful debriefs work only when we have established an environment of trust, safety to be vulnerable, and freedom to share feedback without blame or shame. Leaders must own that responsibility. In addition to debriefing our mistakes, we also need to celebrate accomplishments and successes that we want our team to repeat. The overall focus should remain on improving ourselves and our team. Successful debriefs ensure that we're not so rigid that we can't change our behavior or our way of thinking. The debrief allows us to stay flexible so we are prepared to respond to an evolving environment. When the mission doesn't go as planned, when we make mistakes or have failures, debriefs enable us the space to deconstruct, adapt, and adjust our actions and behaviors going forward.

To do this, we review our mission in detail. We debrief the objectives we set in our flight briefing. If we don't meet one of the objectives, then we drill down to examine why, identify contributing factors, and determine the root cause. Once we understand the root cause, then we talk about lessons learned and the instructional fix. What should have happened? And how can we do it better next time? We walked out of the debrief that day as better pilots, and we shared our lessons with our squadron and pilots around the world. We wanted to be better, and we wanted to help our team perform at their best.

THE AFTERMATH

Once the debrief was done, my squadron commander told me I should call my parents and let them know I was okay. I didn't want to; I wanted to wait until the war was over. I didn't want to bother my parents, to worry them about what had happened. At the time, we were not authorized to use the phone for personal use, so my parents had not heard from me in some time. My commander told me just to call and tell them I was okay, but for security reasons, I could not tell them what happened. So, I called my parents at home in California. It was one o'clock in the morning. I woke them up in the middle of the night and just told them I had a rough day, but I was okay and was happy to be flying the A-10. I told them I loved them and then had to go. My parents later told me they had no idea what to do or think after that call. They looked at each other and wondered how they would ever get back to sleep. The next day, my dad would get some digital pictures sent to him via email from one of his Air Force Academy classmates that further explained the rest of the story.

A few hours later, after debriefing the mission, I walk into the chow hall at our deployed location in Kuwait. I open the door to rows of tables filled with my fellow Airmen and Marines, and suddenly everything seems to go quiet. I feel like they are all looking at me. One of just three female fighter pilots on the base among more than a hundred Air Force and Marine pilots, I already stood out. But now? The word about my landing had gotten out, and now I am even more of an anomaly.

As I wait in line for food, one of the pilots walks up to tell me I had done an impressive job landing the plane. But what he asks me next catches me completely off guard, "So, were you scared?"

I feel like everyone in the room is listening and waiting for me to answer. *Was I scared? Fighter pilots aren't supposed to get scared. We're supposed to be invincible . . . how could I be scared?*

"No, I wasn't scared," I quickly reply. "I didn't have time to be scared."

The reality is, that was a daunting mission; it pushed me to my limits, but it also showed me what I could do. Thankfully, on this day, my training along with grit, fortitude, and a bit of luck came together to help me survive. I knew getting back into the airplane was going to be tough, but I had a job to do, and people were counting on me. I had to face adversity, get over the challenges I encountered, learn from my experiences, and move on. The only certainty of combat is uncertainty, and on this day, I proved to myself that I could manage it.

BACK IN THE AIR

On April 8, 2003, the day after my treacherous combat mission over Baghdad, my flight lead and I were tasked with sitting alert for our combat search and rescue (CSAR) mission. In addition to close air support, CSAR was one of our primary missions during Operation Iraqi Freedom. Our job in the CSAR mission was to assist and coordinate the rescue of a downed pilot by finding their location, then escorting helicopters to come in and pick up the pilot. I had already flown several close air support missions, and now it was our turn to sit alert. In most cases, sitting alert was also a chance to relax and catch up on sleep, which I desperately needed.

We were sitting alert, resting in our alert shack, when the alarm sounded. It was no drill. An A-10 pilot had been shot down near Baghdad. We bolted upright from our cots and sprinted to our jets as quickly as possible, only stopping to get our flight gear on. We raced up the ladders and strapped into the airplane. All other movement on the ramp stopped so we could launch. We made an immediate takeoff and began gathering information about the pilot's location. *Where was he shot down? What was his condition?* We began orchestrating a plan for his rescue. About 30 minutes into our flight, we received a call on the radio, "Sandy flight, you are cleared to RTB (return to base)."

Even though we had been given clear direction, we couldn't turn around right away. We knew we had a pilot on the ground, and we weren't ready to quit so quickly. We pressed on for a few more minutes before the controller relayed that the downed pilot was safe. It turns out, friendly ground forces saw the pilot eject and were able to pick him up. He was safe with American forces. He was also unbelievably lucky.

I never really had time to think about the fact that I was going back to Baghdad where just the day before I had escaped a shoot-down. In my mind, the only thing I could think about was my duty and commitment to this pilot. He was on the ground in enemy territory, and he needed our help. I knew the search and rescue alert crews were there for me the day before, and I was going to do the same for this pilot. This is an extremely important aspect of being a pilot and going into hostile territory. If you are shot down, you know everything possible will be done to get you out.

I wrote my parents and brother an email later that day, knowing they would be worried. I wanted to reassure them I was okay:

> *Mom, Dad, and Alex,*
>
> *I just wanted to send another quick message to let you know that I'm doing fine. It's been a rough few days for the A-10, but we're here doing our job of helping our guys on the ground when they need it most. As I'm sure you've heard on the news, one of our guys had to eject today. He's already back here and doing fine. I have to say that I am very thankful to be flying the Hawg, it's an amazing jet to be so durable. If you want to take a look at the reason I called last night, some pictures have already been posted to the Warthog Territory website. They will probably end up on the news shortly, so I wanted to let you know that the pictures are there if you want to see them. I can't get into specifics, but that should give you some idea of what happened. When our guys on the ground are in trouble, we have to take risks to help them out. I've flown since then and everything was just fine. I'm going to have some good war stories to tell when I get home. I love you all very much and I know how much you have been thinking about me. I know it must be hard for you. Sometimes I wish there was no media over here so you wouldn't have to see so much of what is going on. Then I could just tell you the stories after I'm home. I'm just trying to make sure that you hear from me first, as hard as it may be sometimes. Again, please tell everyone how much I appreciate their thoughts and prayers. I needed them yesterday, and it helped get me back safely.*
>
> *Love, Kim*

Looking back at the letter now, it seems so rigid and formal. I was trying to convince my parents I was okay, but at the same time, I think I was also trying to convince myself. There was still a war going on and I had to compartmentalize what happened and put away the emotions to deal with another time.

Even though I was able to get back in the air the next day, sadly, my aircraft (81–987) never flew again. An aircraft battle damage repair team flew in from Hill Air Force Base to fix the airplane. It wasn't a quick process since more than 600 holes covered the fuselage and tail. The decision was then made to move our aircraft to Tallil Air Base in Iraq so we would be closer to the fight. Unfortunately, that meant the team didn't have time to make all the repairs. Instead, our maintenance team took every part out of the airplane so they would have replacement parts. They took out the engines, the ejection seat, the gun—any part they might need to fix other airplanes, they took it out for spares. Aircraft 987 was then disassembled so it could be shipped home. After a brief stint in the aircraft boneyard, it is now on display at Seymour Johnson Air Force Base in North Carolina.

Eventually, our time in Iraq would come to an end. It was a challenging deployment, but also a defining time in my life. I am thankful for the experience, for having the opportunity to serve my country during a time of war. It also allowed me to prove myself in combat and to establish myself as a capable A-10 pilot early in my career. I put more pressure on myself to succeed than anyone else ever did. I wanted to try harder, work

Figure 7.2 Aircraft 987 being prepared for its trip home to the United States. Although 987 never flew again, I think it had one hell of a final flight.
Photo credit: Technical Sergeant Dave Buttner.

Figure 7.3 Aircraft 987 on display at Seymour-Johnson Air Force Base in North Carolina.
Photo credit: Dr. Roy W. Heidicker.

harder. As a woman, I knew I would stand out, but I wanted to prove I belonged just like everyone else. Fortunately, I proved that I could perform under stress, that I could overcome fear, and I was now a combat-proven warthog pilot.

ACCOUNTABILITY IN LEADERSHIP

Many of the lessons I learned from being a fighter pilot helped me develop as a leader. Seeing the positive impact of a good debrief after a tough mission gave me courage in life and leadership to hold myself and my teammates accountable. I have certainly made my share of mistakes as a leader. It's not easy to admit them, but I have also noticed that I gained respect when I sat down with the team, explained why I had made the decision, then shared that we needed to reassess and find a better way. What we were doing wasn't working, and we needed to come up with a new solution. I tried to get my team's point of view and ask what ideas they had to improve. I also appreciated when my team had the courage to give me candid feedback, to let me know when they didn't understand something, or to let me know that something wasn't working.

We need to have the courage to take responsibility for our actions and give feedback to our team when they don't meet expectations. Providing feedback can be difficult, especially when you're letting someone know they're not meeting expectations. For me, it's one of the most difficult aspects of being a leader. Those conversations aren't fun, but they are necessary. Just as with flying, we owe it to our team to provide feedback, to recommend course corrections, and to let people know when they're not making the cut.

In 2016, I took command of the 612th Theater Operations Group and the 474th Air Expeditionary Group. The mission was unique. I would provide command and control of forces assigned to Air Forces Southern as they conducted operations in the Southern Command Area of Responsibility. Southern Command, or SOUTHCOM, is responsible for providing contingency planning, operations, and security cooperation in Central America, South America, and the Caribbean. According to SOUTHCOM, its mission is to deter aggression, defeat threats, rapidly respond to crises, and build regional capacity, working with our allies, partner nations, and US government team members to enhance security and defend the US homeland and our national interests.

As the Operations Group Commander, I was responsible for our permanent party airmen located at Davis-Monthan Air Force Base in Arizona, as well as our airmen overseas located in Honduras, Curacao, and Colombia. As the Expeditionary Group Commander, I was responsible for airmen who deployed to the region. My airmen were spread from Guantanamo Bay in Cuba to Belize, El Salvador, and Panama in Central America, as well as Peru in South America. At the peak of operations, I was responsible for more than 1,000 personnel. Mission sets varied from counterdrug operations to humanitarian assistance and disaster relief to detention operations. It was a complex set of missions.

After about a year into my command tour, I was on one of my routine trips to Guantanamo Bay when my airmen asked to meet with me without the squadron commander in the room. He was their supervisor, so this was an unusual request, and it got my attention. We sat down in one of the tents with the team and they raised some concerns they had with his leadership. They were open and honest with me, and I was thankful they trusted me with their feedback. My airmen were concerned about the safety of their team because the squadron commander was asking them to do things they weren't trained to do. He was also imposing rules on them he wasn't following himself. When his senior non-commissioned officers (mid-level leadership) and junior officers tried to give him feedback, he repeatedly said he didn't agree with their assessment. They were concerned and frustrated, and morale was at an all-time low.

After meeting with the team, I sat down to talk with the squadron commander to get his point of view. I approached it as a mentoring session, hoping I could improve the situation. As we discussed the concerns and issues, he seemed disinterested in changing his ways and often seemed unaware of the problems he was having with his team even though some of the non-commissioned officers and junior officers had already approached him with these same concerns. When your senior enlisted team, as well as your junior officers, come to you with a problem about your leadership, then it's time to sit down and listen. Hear them out. Maybe you think you're doing a respectable job, but when there's a lot of feedback to the contrary, then it might be time to accept their assessment and take a new approach. Unfortunately, he wasn't interested in that, and as a result he had completely lost their trust.

I left my team in Guantanamo after that visit with a pit in my stomach. I talked to the senior leadership at Guantanamo to make them aware of my concerns. I also talked to my three-star boss at home and walked him through what was going on. Over the next week, I continued to get emails about safety concerns and morale issues, and I knew I had to act. I could not let this continue. As hard as it was to do, I felt in my gut that removing him from command was the right decision. I respected his expertise in the field, but he did not have the skills to lead his team of airmen.

Relaying the news to him was one of the most difficult conversations I have had with one of my airmen. I don't like delivering bad news and this was definitely bad news. At the same time, I had a responsibility to take care of him as a person. I did my best to explain the situation to him and help him understand why I made the decision. He was angry. A part of me felt like I had failed him as his commander in trying to help him improve as a leader. Unfortunately, there just wasn't time. I could not risk the safety of my airmen.

Sometimes leaders have to make tough calls, decisions we know will have an impact on people's lives. We owe it to our team because they are counting on us. On my next trip to Guantanamo, I was overwhelmed by the response from my team. They were appreciative that I had acted, that I trusted them, and that I was willing to act swiftly even though it would have been easier to just let him finish out his command tour. A few months later, the senior leadership at Guantanamo released an investigation report regarding the climate in his unit, which detailed a toxic work environment. Although it was a difficult decision, I had made the right choice.

In his book, *Call Sign Chaos*, General Jim Mattis expresses the tension associated with relieving someone from command. He says, "You know how hard dedicated officers have worked, and you know what the effect of relief will be, upon them, their families, and their troops. . . But I would be remiss if I did not address the necessity to relieve someone from command, because it is so fundamental to leadership. We learn most about ourselves when things go wrong."[1] This was a learning situation for me, too. From a leadership perspective, I felt I had failed my squadron commander. If I could have just known sooner, recognized the signs sooner, then maybe I could have helped by giving him feedback earlier on and mentoring him along the way. This was one of the most difficult leadership situations I have dealt with throughout my career, but I learned a lot in the process and believe it's important to share the experience.

CONSIDERATIONS FOR LEADERS

Teams want leaders who will deliver consistent results, are trustworthy and transparent, will make tough decisions, and are willing to lead by example. To be an effective leader, we must hold team members accountable, and we must hold ourselves accountable too. So, how do we cultivate a culture of accountability in our organizations?

- Create an environment of trust where accountability is both expected and desired.
- Request feedback from superiors, peers, and subordinates. Rather than being defensive, be receptive to feedback. Truly listen to what people are saying, and look for ways to improve.
- Be open to better ways of executing the mission. Model that it's okay to adjust a course of action.
- Admit mistakes. Own any missteps and gain credibility in the process. If we set the example, then our team is more likely to own up to errors and even identify minor issues sooner before they become significant for the organization.

Credibility, both personal and professional, is essential for leaders. If a team doesn't believe in their leader, they will not be as effective and are unlikely to put forward their best effort. Accountability requires courage, and it also ensures our team will perform at their best. ***If you want to lead with courage, then take ownership of your actions and create a culture where mistakes and failures are opportunities for improvement.***

Chapter 8

AVIATE, NAVIGATE, COMMUNICATE

"Action expresses priorities."

—Mahatma Gandhi

Figure 8.1 Preparing to launch on a combat mission. Over the course of my career, I flew 121 combat missions over Iraq and Afghanistan.

PRIORITIZING EFFECTIVELY

"Aviate, navigate, and communicate" is a simple phrase we learn early in pilot training that helps us get through a demanding situation. When we face an emergency, we learn to slow down and focus on what's most important first: maintaining control of the airplane. Then we navigate, gaining situational awareness of what is going on around us and figuring out where we need to go. From there, we communicate, letting others know about the problem and requesting assistance if required from our wingmen or other assets. This simple phrase helps pilots prioritize under pressure and maintain focus on the most important aspects first.

When my jet was hit over Baghdad, I didn't have time to open a checklist or to ask for help, I had to react immediately. Thankfully, my training kicks in and I am able to respond and act during this extremely stressful situation. I have to focus on what is most important first. This means getting my airplane under control. Even though I am task-saturated with multiple problems, my primary task is to keep the jet flying. I can't just stop flying the airplane while I figure out what to do.

Next, I need situational awareness of my surroundings. To navigate I have to figure out where I am and where I need to go. If I have to eject, I want to be over a friendly location, so I need to get my airplane there quickly. I also have to be aware of the enemy threats in the area and do my best to avoid them.

Finally, I have to communicate to let my flight lead know what happened so he can help. My communication needs to be clear, concise, and correct in such a critical moment.

The simple phrase "aviate, navigate, communicate" helps us prioritize and focus during difficult moments. Too often in an emergency, pilots become overly focused on a problem and they forget to fly the airplane. The consequences of not following this procedure can be deadly. In 1972, pilots flying an Eastern Airlines jumbo jet on approach to Miami International Airport became so focused on a failed landing gear light that they forgot to fly the airplane. They failed to notice that the autopilot was accidentally disconnected. In just two minutes, the airplane began a gradual descent that went unnoticed by the flight crew. The aircraft eventually crashed in the everglades, resulting in 101 fatalities. The accident investigation concluded that "preoccupation with a malfunction of the nose landing gear position indicating system distracted the crew's attention from the instruments and allowed the descent to go unnoticed."[1] It was a tragic accident and one that sadly could have been avoided by following the straightforward process of aviating, navigating, and communicating.

CALM IN THE STORM

In early 2005, the 75th Fighter Squadron was tasked to return to Afghanistan for another six-month deployment to support Operation Enduring Freedom. I was now an experienced instructor pilot in the squadron and would be part of a 12-ship of A-10s that would take off from Pope Air Force Base in North Carolina and fly across the pond to Afghanistan. We would make a few stops along the way for pilot rest and to allow maintenance an opportunity to look at our airplanes. After a night of rest at Naval Air Station Sigonella in Italy, we took off uneventfully but ran into problems after rejoining with our first tanker. Two of our aircraft were unable to refuel and would need to return to Sigonella until maintenance could fix the airplanes. In total, four of us would return to Sigonella to maintain flight integrity and provide mutual support. However, due to a delay in getting parts to fix the airplanes, as well as diplomatic clearance issues, we would end up spending two weeks in Sigonella before I led the final four-ship of A-10s from Sigonella Air Base to Afghanistan.

The mission to Afghanistan was straightforward, but the weather was not. At the time, controlling agencies were at a minimum and our primary plan was to stay out of the clouds and follow visual flight rules, meaning we would be able to see other aircraft and avoid them. Unfortunately, the weather had other plans. As we made our way into Afghanistan, the clouds and weather got worse. We climbed higher and higher to get out of the weather, but we reached the point where we could not fly any higher (for fear of losing an engine), and still, we could not get out of the weather. My wingmen were behind me in trail formation, essentially a line of aircraft with each aircraft about a mile apart from the aircraft in front of them. It wasn't ideal, but the weather required flexibility. We made the standard radio reporting calls as required by the procedures for this type of situation, but it was still uncomfortable being in the weather without radar to help us identify nearby aircraft. Everything was going smoothly until we were about 100 miles south of Bagram Air Base when I lost radio communication with my number four airplane.

"Hawg 4, radio check," I asked over the radio, inviting him to respond.

"Hawg 4, this is Hawg 1, how do you read?" I asked again.

"Hawg 4 status?" I questioned, now growing more nervous about the situation.

Still nothing. I asked Hawg 3 to see if he could raise Hawg 4 since he was closer to him in formation.

Silence.

No matter what we tried, we could not get Hawg 4 on the radio on any frequency. I continued trying to reach him while also coordinating approaches for my other wingmen. Was he simply NORDO (no radio) or did something worse happen? High mountains surrounded Bagram Air Base so if you went off the prescribed air track, it could be deadly.

In the first few minutes of not being able to reach Hawg 4, I became overly fixated on trying to reach him. I knew my other wingmen were nervous, too. What had happened to number four? Would we all be able to land safely? I soon realized that focusing on one aircraft was distracting me from keeping the other three airplanes safe. I had to give that task to someone else in the flight or I would not be able to focus on my main priority of leading the formation. Even though I was worried about the status of Hawg 4, I still had the responsibility of getting the other three aircraft on the ground safely. I prioritized my actions to help me remain calm.

Aviate—fly my own airplane.

Navigate—ensure we have a safe path down to the runway at Bagram Air Base.

Communicate—continue to communicate with my four-ship as well as the air traffic controllers on the ground to keep everyone informed and to see what they could do to help.

Eventually, as we got lower in altitude, we finally heard a faint call over the radio from Hawg 4. I was beyond relieved to hear his voice. I could not fathom losing one of my wingmen. No matter what happened, I would still feel responsible. I was leading the formation and their safety was my responsibility. Thankfully, we only had a faulty radio to report on landing.

There will be times when leaders will feel overwhelmed due to competing priorities. We will face moments of stress, and we must do our best to remain calm and focus on what's most important first. We must be able to aviate, navigate, and communicate.

Figure 8.2 Arriving at Bagram Air Base, Afghanistan, after leading my four-ship of A-10s through significant weather on our approach.

LEADING IN A CRISIS

In July 2020, I became the director of the Center for Character and Leadership Development at the United States Air Force Academy in the middle of a pandemic. The Academy had just started bringing cadets back to the Academy after sending the lower three classes home in March and graduating the first-class cadets six weeks early in April. Now, we had a requirement to bring in a new class of cadets to meet congressionally mandated requirements. Academy leadership had to find a way to conduct Basic Cadet Training during the pandemic with more than 1,000 new cadets on base. To meet this requirement, we brought back limited numbers of upper-class cadets to run basic training and put strict procedures in place to avoid a coronavirus outbreak. Cadets were restricted to base and had limited contact with staff and faculty who lived off base and were primarily operating remotely. It was a tough time to begin as a new leader in an organization where I didn't know the team.

As the new director, I wanted to spend time with my team and connect with them on a more personal level. Thanks to the remote environment, I couldn't achieve this in the way I had done in the past. People were working from home, and we only had our mission-essential personnel in the building. It was a challenging time to meet and connect with people, but I had to work with the situation and not fight against it. I decided to take the time to meet with my team virtually, attempting to get to know them through the computer screen. I listened to their concerns and struggles, not just with work but also with the demanding pandemic world we were all trying to survive in. I learned quickly that there were competing priorities and interests as well as frustration that there was too much to do and not enough hours in the day to get it done. If I was going to make any progress and lead effectively, I was going to have to go back to the basics to help my team prioritize their actions under the enormous pressure of competing demands. It was back to aviate, navigate, and communicate.

When a crisis hits (like a pandemic), we aviate by keeping our team on course and maintaining focus on our critical priorities. There are the things that we have to keep doing, or we will fail. Then we navigate. We must be aware of the goals we are trying to achieve even in a crisis, forging a clear path for our team by knowing where there are threats or risks to them or the mission. And finally, we must communicate clearly and concisely to our team to ensure they know the way forward and to communicate with leadership when we need help. Communication can be challenging in large organizations. There are often concerns that we're not communicating enough, not getting information out fast enough, or the information isn't reaching the lower levels. This can be a constant battle unless we encourage leadership at all levels to get out and talk to their teams and empower them to share information.

In times of crisis, leaders must be able to focus on critical priorities, keeping our team on course. We must also help our team prioritize their efforts. We must be clear about our priorities and help our team focus on what's most important first.

CONTROL VERSUS INFLUENCE

There are things in life we can control, things we can influence, and things that we can't control or influence. If we focus first on those things we can control, then we can leave the rest for later or not spend time on them at all.

As A-10 pilots, when we are called in to provide close air support, the mission can be complicated due to multiple competing factors, such as weather, threats, and pressure to perform to save lives. There are many factors we must take into consideration as we develop our plan to tackle the complexity of the tactical problem. To be effective, we must first focus on what we can control. We formulate a plan to limit threats and reduce risk while also meeting our mission objectives. Although the situation can be complex and can sometimes feel overwhelming, like the odds are against us, we must focus on our priorities and those things we can control. Yes, the weather might be a concern, but we have no control or influence over the weather, so we create a plan to work around it. If we are going to be effective, we can't spend time worrying about things we cannot control or influence. We have to focus our efforts on the areas where we know we can make a difference.

These prioritization concepts work when dealing with complex problems in the air and on the ground as we struggle to prioritize our time and energy. Today, as I lead my team, I focus most of my efforts on what I can control. Then, I spend the remaining time working on areas that I can influence. Although I remain aware of other areas where I might have concerns, if I don't have control or influence over them, I don't spend my time there. Dr. Angela Duckworth, professor of psychology and best-selling author of the book *Grit: The Power of Passion and Persever-ance*, says that gritty people in challenging times focus on the things they have some control over and at the same time acknowledge the things they have no control over. By focusing on what we can control, especially in challenging circumstances, we can more accurately prioritize and experi-ence less stress.

CONSIDERATIONS FOR LEADERS

There were many times throughout my career when I felt inundated by competing demands and priorities. I've also had moments when I didn't even know where to start, feeling like there was no way possible to get eve-rything done. Sometimes it can be overwhelming when we have a lot of information to process, problems to think through, and issues to confront. In these instances, try to do the following:

- Prioritize tasks based on urgency and importance.
- Focus on those things in your control. Communicate priorities to teammates.
- Do those things that only you can do and delegate lower-level tasks to team members as needed.

It takes courage to lead in a crisis. It can feel overwhelming with mul-tiple competing priorities. However, if we focus on what's most important first, then we can lead our team successfully in the face of challenges. *If you want to lead with courage, then aviate, navigate, and commu-nicate. Learn to prioritize under pressure and focus on what's most important first.*

Chapter 9

RECOGNIZE, CONFIRM, RECOVER

"Whether outwardly or inwardly, whether in space or time, the farther we penetrate the unknown, the vaster and more marvelous it becomes."

—Charles Lindbergh

Figure 9.1 75th Expeditionary Fighter Squadron, Bagram Air Base, Afghanistan, during Operation Enduring Freedom.

INTO THE UNKNOWN

Life at Bagram Air Base in Afghanistan in 2005 was drastically different from my first experience there in 2002. I walked into the Air Force compound and was shocked to see the change from a few wide-open tents to a substantial compound with hard billets, tents on the inside with plywood frames on the outside for additional protection. In 2002, I was in one tent with officers and enlisted men and women. I stared at the sign on the outside of my tent that proclaimed, "Female Officers." I would now unfortunately be separated from my squadron. Another big change was that there were no longer Afghans on the base working in our facilities since the United States had closed work access to the base due to security concerns. There were a lot more rules and regulations. We had to wear reflective belts everywhere we went because there were now so many vehicles on the base. There were some positive changes in living conditions, too. Instead of MREs (meals ready to eat), we now had chow halls and even a base exchange where we could buy supplies, coffee, or burgers. Over the two and a half years since our last deployment, our fellow A-10 pilots had built up a lounge area that boasted an alcohol-free bar made

131

from scrap wood and colorful couches and chairs acquired from the local Afghan bazaar. It was a great place to regroup, relax, and destress after a combat mission.

Since I was now an experienced A-10 instructor pilot in the squadron and this was my second deployment to Afghanistan, I would be leading missions to support troops on the ground, which varied from close air support missions to convoy escort missions. We had to be prepared to face the unknown. When we were on alert, we had to be ready for just about anything, anywhere in Afghanistan. Alert missions were always exciting because we never knew when the call would come or what we would be tasked to do. We had to be ready at a moment's notice. We carried radios with us wherever we went and had a pickup truck to get us to the flight line as fast as possible. Our crew chiefs always had the jets ready to go so we could launch as soon as we arrived. We carried maps for the entire country stuffed in the nose of our cockpit so we could ensure we were prepared for wherever the next firefight erupted. Usually, we would be launched to support a close air support mission, but occasionally, we would get a mission that surprised us.

HUMANITARIAN HAWG

On March 29, 2005, my wingman and I were tasked with sitting alert. We were having lunch in the chow hall when the call came over the radio, "Alert Launch, Alert Launch." There was no time to clean up our trays of food; we grabbed our gear and ran out to the truck. My wingman drove while I talked with our operations desk about what they knew about our mission. We expected to hear about coalition forces in trouble and under attack from the enemy. Not today. The Band Sultan Dam in a town south of Bagram called Ghazni had burst due to a huge inflow of water from melted snow. We were tasked to go look for survivors, an unexpected humanitarian mission for the A-10.

We parked the truck next to the jets, and hopped out, briefly stopping to put on our G-suits, harnesses, and survival vests, which were hanging on the jet's wing. We ran up the ladder, started engines, and we were off. As soon as we got airborne, we began gathering as much information about our mission as possible. Reports relayed that the floodwaters had already killed at least 20 people, destroying hundreds of houses and displacing thousands. I was afraid of what we would find when we arrived on station.

Our mission was to first look for survivors and direct helicopters to their position so they could execute a rescue mission. As we flew overhead the dam and surrounding areas, we could see the devastation. We set up in a stack over the area so I could fly low and look for survivors while my wingman held high to look for potential threats in the area. As I cruised over the area, I could see Afghans isolated on small heaps of land now surrounded by water. I also saw homes completely washed away. It was devastating to see so much destruction in a country that had already faced so much hardship.

Once we were confident there were no other isolated survivors and the rescue helicopters no longer required our assistance, we began our next task. Higher headquarters tasked us to look at the damage to the dam with the use of our targeting pod so we could measure the extent of the damage and provide a video of the damaged area. It was a nontraditional use of an airplane designed for close air support.

Over several days, Afghan and coalition forces airlifted hundreds of stranded Afghans to safety throughout the flooded region. In response to this unconventional mission, Colonel Warren Henderson, the 455th Expeditionary Operations Group Commander, said, "This mission took the Hog to an all-new level. We've always carried out Combat Search

Figure 9.2 A-10 Alert Crew at Bagram Air Base, Afghanistan. We decided to make our alert truck look like an A-10 by mounting a gun on the front.

and Rescue, but we're definitely conducting more nontraditional roles here in Afghanistan . . . in this case, using the A-10's pinpoint accuracy to save lives versus take lives." It turns out we did well on the nontraditional humanitarian assistance and disaster relief mission.

UNUSUAL ATTITUDE

After a few weeks of flying during the day, I switched to night operations. It was remarkable flying at night in a place with so few lights. It was extraordinarily dark and could be disorienting without a horizon. It was so dark that we learned to air refuel wearing night-vision goggles (NVGs) to help us find the tanker and connect with the boom.

On what seemed like one of the darkest nights in Afghanistan with intermittent cloud cover dotting the sky, I rejoined with the tanker and refueled without issue. While moving away from the tanker after disconnecting, I became severely disoriented. It seemed like every way I looked, I continued to see the lights from the tanker. It was like they were reflecting off every surface and I couldn't figure out what was real and what was a reflection. I tried to move away from the light of the tanker, but no matter what I did, I felt like I just kept getting closer to the tanker. I was worried I was going to crash into it, which would have been catastrophic for everyone. I keyed the mic, "1s, spatially disoriented, getting away."

I quickly took off my NVGs and did my best to pull away from the tanker. It turns out I had rolled inverted and barrel-rolled my airplane around the tanker and ended up on the other side, but now farther away. I stared at my instruments, willing them to tell me the truth. "Recognize, confirm, recover."

The lack of visual cues when in weather can cause a pilot to become spatially disoriented, losing the ability to determine their position in relation to the horizon. "Sight, supported by other senses, allows a pilot to maintain orientation while flying. However, when visibility is restricted (i.e., no visual reference to the horizon or surface detected) the body's supporting senses can conflict with what is seen."[1] When spatial disorientation occurs, sensory conflicts and optical illusions often make it difficult for a pilot to tell which way is up, occasionally resulting in an unusual attitude in the aircraft. An unusual attitude in an airplane is commonly referenced as an unintended or unexpected attitude, which is an aircraft's position in relation to the horizon (a known reference). The correct response to an unusual attitude is to recognize, confirm, and recover. Recognizing an unusual attitude is critical to a successful recovery. Then, a pilot must confirm that an unusual attitude exists by confirming our attitude with both our primary and secondary flight instruments. Recovery actions should then be compatible with the severity of the unusual attitude.

In my situation, I knew I was disoriented. I was just trying to get my brain to confirm what right-side-up looked like, then make my hands execute the correct recovery control inputs. I eventually confirmed my aircraft attitude by looking at my flight instruments and was able to recover by trusting my flight instruments and taking the appropriate action. Finally, the gyros inside my brain eventually re-caged and my position in the sky became clear. But that initial feeling of being overwhelmed by a completely unusual and unexpected situation rocked my confidence. I had to go back to the basics, trust my instruments, and take the appropriate action to recover and correct the situation.

CONFIRMATION IS CRITICAL

Combat can be volatile, uncertain, complex, and ambiguous. A-10 pilots holding overhead have a responsibility to handle the unexpected, to respond and adapt under stress. When an unusual or uncertain situation arises, it's my responsibility as the flight lead to sort it out, recognize what's going on, confirm the details, come up with a plan, and act based on the severity of the situation.

One hot afternoon in Afghanistan, we launched on alert to assist with the rescue and recovery of an injured high-ranking Afghan soldier. We only had general coordinates for the location of the village where the special forces team was hunkered down with our Afghan partners, but not much else. The medical evacuation assets were enroute but would take longer to arrive on station. The special forces team wanted A-10s overhead to provide protection while they waited for the helicopters. As we approached the village, we made radio contact with the ground team and could hear the urgency in their voices. The Afghan soldier was not doing well, could not be moved, and the enemy was closing in on their position. We held overhead the village while the ground controller gave us a talk-on to their position. Many of the buildings in the village looked the same and we had to be certain of their position in case we needed to put fire down on the enemy. I followed his talk-on.

"Hawg 1, call contact on the 4-way intersection on the east side of the village," the ground controller directed.

"Contact," came my reply.

"Come five houses north of the intersection and tell me what you see," he directed.

I quickly responded with what I could see: "There appears to be an open courtyard with a house on the north side of the courtyard."

"We are in the house north of that courtyard. That's the friendly position," he emphasized.

"I am visual the friendly position," I responded.

The talk-on conversation between a ground controller and a pilot is a sequence of description and confirmation. We're constantly going back and forth to make sure we are communicating clearly and confirming what we see. The view from the air can be drastically different from the view on the ground, so we must have confirmation we are looking at the same position.

"Two, confirm you followed the talk-on and are visual the friendly location?" I asked my wingman.

"Confirm the friendly building is rectangle in shape and is oriented east-west?" he asked.

"Affirm," I replied on the radio.

I discussed our plan with my wingman so we could protect the friendly troops on the ground while also protecting the inbound helicopters. I trusted his experience and expertise. I decided I would hold above the friendly position and my wingman would rejoin with the helicopters to support them as they approached the landing zone where they would be most vulnerable. As I relayed my plan to my wingman, he confirmed that he thought it was the best course of action based on the situation.

"Hawg 1, request a show of force 200 meters west of our position," the ground controller said firmly over the radio. "We need it now."

I immediately dumped my nose at the ground, quickly gaining speed, leveling out at our minimum altitude, and dumping flares out of my aircraft. From the ground, it was loud and forceful. And then, we lost all contact with the ground team. Our radios went silent. The helicopters were inbound. *Do we abort, or do we continue?* If we aborted, the Afghan soldier would likely die. If we continued, we could be setting our helicopters up for an ambush. I quickly discussed the situation with the helicopter mission commander and my wingman who was escorting them into the landing zone. They could see the landing zone ahead, and my wingman was conducting a racetrack pattern around the helicopters to provide additional firepower. I was covering down on the friendly location, ready to roll in on the enemy as needed. We all confirmed we were in position and ready. We would continue the mission as planned. Because we were all looking at the same objective with a different viewpoint, our communication helped us confirm our approach and plan of action in the face of uncertainty.

Within minutes, the helicopters landed safely, the special forces team loaded the Afghan soldier, and he was on his way to the nearest Forward Operating Base. There were no other casualties.

FACING THE UNEXPECTED

Years later, when I was selected for group command, I was excited and nervous about the opportunity. I was a highly experienced A-10 pilot and had already commanded at the squadron level, but this was a completely different environment. I wasn't leading A-10 pilots anymore, I was now leading civil engineers, lawyers, firefighters, air traffic controllers, and security forces. I wasn't an expert in any of these fields. To say that I felt out of my element was an understatement. But the leadership principles that had worked in the past helped me prepare for this unique leadership opportunity.

As a new commander, I recognized I was in unfamiliar territory. Instead of close air support missions, I was now responsible for counter-drug operations, humanitarian missions, and building partnership capacity in South America, Central America, and the Caribbean. These were new missions in new locations. My immediate plan was to reach out to my team, get smart on the environment, and get their view on the situations they were facing in their areas of responsibility. This would be a repeated occurrence throughout my time in command as I continued to face new and often unexpected situations. When my team gave me feedback or ideas based on their experience, I trusted their expertise; then based on all the information, I could decide on the best way forward.

Recognize, confirm, recover. It works in an airplane, and it works in leadership, too. I recognized I was in unfamiliar territory. I confirmed plans, policies, and procedures with trusted members of my team. I recovered by taking the best action required for the situation and gained confidence in the process, too.

CONSIDERATIONS FOR LEADERS

In dynamic and volatile environments, leaders play a critical role in bringing clarity in the face of uncertainty. Leaders need to be able to thrive when faced with unfamiliar or unexpected situations. When confronted with an "unusual attitude,"' we can regain control when we recognize, confirm, and recover.

- Recognize (and admit) the situation exists. It can be hard to admit we're in an unknown situation, especially when we feel unprepared.
- Confirm the situation with trusted members of the team. What is their perception? Are there recommendations on a way forward or is outside help needed?
- Recover by taking the best action based on the situation and information available.

In today's complex environment, filled with uncertainty and ambiguity, we need leaders who can perform in the face of the unknown. We'll likely never have perfect information or the perfect solution. Recognize what you don't have, confirm the minimum information needed, and then execute. *If you want to lead with courage, then bring clarity and confidence in the face of uncertainty. Recognize, confirm, recover.*

Chapter 10

COMMAND AND CONNECTION

"Courage and fear are not mutually exclusive. Most of us feel brave and afraid at the exact same time."

—Brené Brown

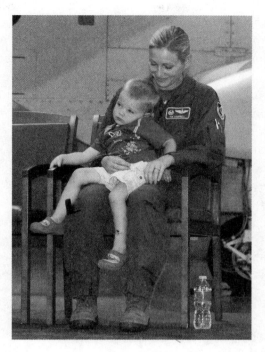

Figure 10.1 My change of command ceremony, taking command of the 355th Operations Support Squadron at Davis-Monthan Air Force Base in Arizona. My son decided he would prefer to sit with me on stage.

HUMBLE, APPROACHABLE, CREDIBLE

As I was learning to be a young leader in the Air Force, I had the opportunity to be trained and mentored by our weapons officer, Captain (now Brigadier General) Mike "Johnny Bravo" Drowley. When Johnny Bravo arrived at the 75th Fighter Squadron, he was recently graduated from Weapons School and had an immense amount of expertise and experience. The motto at the Air Force Weapons School, the Air Force equivalent to TOPGUN, is to be humble, approachable, and credible. He taught me the tactics, techniques, and procedures of how to lead a four-ship of A-10s, but more important, he taught me how to lead with humility and approachability. Johnny Bravo set the example for all of us. When I was upgrading to become an instructor in the A-10, he spent hours of his time sitting down with all the new instructors in the squadron, helping us to improve. He was always available for a phone call

141

to discuss attack geometry and tactics. It's no surprise that credibility was essential to being a flight lead or instructor in the A-10 but being humble and approachable was something new. Most often fighter pilots aren't perceived as humble. I've frequently heard the terms *cocky* and *arrogant* instead. But in this case, the best fighter pilots in the squadron had three identifiable traits. They were humble. They were approachable. And they were credible.

When we think about leadership, we may think that characteristics like humility, approachability, and vulnerability can be signs of weakness. Sometimes we go into a new leadership opportunity thinking we have to put on a tough exterior in order to prove our credibility and capability. I believe the opposite is true. Yes, credibility is essential, but the best leaders I've worked for and with have shown vulnerability by being humble and approachable. I learned these traits early in my flying career, and they have stayed with me as I've taken on new leadership opportunities in my military career and beyond.

THE HUMAN SIDE OF LEADERSHIP

One of the greatest privileges that comes from being an officer in the profession of arms is the opportunity to command. My first opportunity to command a squadron came in June 2011. I was selected to lead the 355th Operations Support Squadron, a squadron of more than 150 airmen, tasked to run the airfield, provide intelligence, maintain aircrew flight equipment, and conduct daily scheduling and training operations for the entire wing of A-10 pilots at Davis-Monthan Air Force Base. I was excited for the opportunity to lead my airmen, but I was nervous, too, because it was now *my* opportunity to lead and set the example.

A formal change of command ceremony commemorates the beginning of a command tour. My ceremony was held in an aircraft hangar out on the flight line. The hangar was full of guests, including members of my soon-to-be squadron standing in formation, senior leadership from the base, friends and family who had flown in from around the country to attend, as well as local city officials. It was a big, formal event. I was sitting on stage with the outgoing commander as well as my new boss who was officiating the ceremony. Behind me, a clean and shiny A-10. My husband and my three-year-old son were sitting in the front row to watch the ceremony.

About 15 minutes into the ceremony, I looked down at my son, who I could tell by this point was completely bored out of his mind. He looked up at me, looked at my husband, and then to our surprise, stood up. *What is he going to do?*

My commander was giving a speech about the importance of our mission and having a good leader, but I could barely focus on what he was saying. My son started taking slow, small steps, as if he moved slowly enough, he would be essentially invisible and nobody would notice. I noticed. My husband noticed. We were looking at each other, silently communicating, trying to figure out what we were going to do. My husband was concerned that if he tried to make my son sit back down, we might have a full-blown temper tantrum in the front row. And I was of course looking at him like . . . *please do something! What is everyone going to think?*

A few more steps. *Maybe he will stop at the base of the stairs and sit down.* A few more steps. He looked at me, looked at the stairs . . . one step, two steps. And now he was on the stage. I was trying to keep a straight face and listen to what my boss was saying. *What is my team going to think of me? She can't even control her three-year-old son and she's supposed to lead this squadron?*

A few more steps. And then he hopped right up in my lap. There wasn't much I could do at this point but look down at him and smile. He was content to stay there with me and enjoy the view from the stage.

I worried about what my airmen would think of their new commander . . . this wasn't proper military protocol. But then as I looked down at my son, totally content to be in the comfort of my lap, I realized it was best my airmen saw me as human, too. And just like everyone in that hangar, I wasn't perfect and I had my own challenges.

At that moment sitting up on stage with my son in my lap, even though I was nervous about what my team would think, I decided to let them see me for who I was. I was a mom, a fighter pilot, a wife, and a leader. It was difficult to let them see me for all those things, but that's the human side of leadership. We can be strong and we can be compassionate at the same time. We can be tough and we can be kind.

Being vulnerable and showing the human side of leadership isn't a weakness. Vulnerable leadership is being open to risk and uncertainty. It's admitting we don't have all the answers and listening to our team for ideas. It's making a mistake or a bad decision and then stepping up to own it. All these actions help establish an environment of trust and set the stage for greater creativity and innovation in our organization. Even though it may not be easy, vulnerability in leadership is critical to creating connections with our team and opening opportunities for even greater success.

In an article for *Harvard Business Review*, Harvard lecturer and social psychologist Dr. Amy Cuddy discusses the growing body of research that suggests that the way to influence — and to lead — is to begin with warmth, which includes trustworthiness and approachability. Dr. Cuddy says that prioritizing warmth helps you connect immediately with those around you, demonstrating that you hear them, understand them, and can be trusted by them.[1] To me, this means showing the human side of leadership and making time to get to know our team, to understand what they do and how they contribute to the organization. We need to show our team that we value their expertise, that they have a critical role in the organization.

In the next few days after my change of command ceremony, I spent time walking around and getting to know my team. I was still nervous about what my team was thinking about my son getting up in my lap and what they might say. It turns out, it was the highlight of the ceremony for many of them because it made me human. My airmen taught me a lesson that day, too. We can earn trust by being vulnerable.

GO INTO THE BURN HOUSE

In 2016, when I became a group commander, responsible for more than 1,000 personnel, these ideas on vulnerable leadership were amplified. Group command was a privilege in that I had a greater impact, but it was also a challenge because now my decisions had much larger ramifications. Unlike squadron command, where I had the opportunity to get to know and connect with everyone, this was a much larger group. I no longer had a direct connection with all my airmen because there were a lot more of them and also because they were spread over thousands of miles and rotated frequently. I had to rely on and trust my squadron commanders (my direct reports) to take care of their airmen in each location. I was excited for the opportunity to make an impact and difference on a much larger scale, also knowing that my decisions could now have strategic-level implications.

Despite the size and distance of my squadrons, it was important for me to get out and meet my airmen, to understand their missions, and to know where I needed to advocate for them to ensure they had the resources to do their jobs. After a few weeks into my command tour, I traveled to meet with my airmen at Soto Cano Air Base, a Honduran military base located in central Honduras. I arrived at the International Airport in Tegucigalpa, which is ranked as the second most extreme airport in the world based on its harrowing approach to the runway through high terrain. After surviving the treacherous approach and landing safely in Tegucigalpa, my team met me at international arrivals, and we began the almost two-hour drive through the mountains to Soto Cano Air Base. According to the Department of Defense, the base is composed of more than 500 US military personnel (as part of Joint Task Force Bravo) and more than 500 US and Honduran civilians. Joint Task Force Bravo is one of three task forces under United States Southern Command. Joint Task Force Bravo operates a forward airbase, organizes multilateral exercises, and supports, in cooperation with our partner nations, counter-transnational organized crime missions, humanitarian assistance/disaster relief efforts, and promotes cooperation and security in the region.

We pulled onto the base guarded by the Honduran military, did a quick uniform change, and I began my first visit with the 612th Air Base Squadron. The squadron's mission is to provide airbase support to Joint Task Force Bravo, including air traffic control, logistics, base civil engineering, fire fighting, airfield operations, and personnel functions. I first checked in with the firefighters and told them I wanted to know more about what they did, what concerns they had, and to hear what they liked about their jobs. My fire chief looked at me, smiled, and said, "Ma'am, the best way for you to appreciate our mission is to suit up and go into the burn house with us."

I was a little conflicted with this idea. I'm a fighter pilot, and we like to avoid fires. This was way outside my comfort zone. The last thing I wanted was to do something stupid in front of my airmen. But the benefit was doing something with my airmen where I could learn from them, to put my trust in them. Sometimes we have to show trust to earn trust. It was an opportunity to connect with them in their own element and on their own turf. I also knew that by putting on that suit and going into the burn house with them, I would better understand their mission. I didn't take much time to deliberate. I set my ego aside. It was about doing something I wasn't comfortable doing, doing something I knew I could fail.

And my airmen knew that; they knew this wasn't my area of expertise, but they respected that I was willing to try.

We went into the firehouse to get the safety briefing. The fire chief let one of my young airmen give me the briefing, and I listened to every word. After the briefing, we went out to practice with some of the gear. I still felt nervous because I knew everyone was watching me. Then the alarm sounded. Practice time was over. I attempted to get my gear on as fast as I could (which was not fast at all) and got everything checked by another young airman to ensure I would be protected once we got into the burn house. We hopped into the fire truck, and with sirens blaring raced over to the burn house.

As we approached, I could see smoke starting to rise out of the building. We jumped out, linked up, and stood at the door. My heart was racing, adrenaline pumping. I was standing in front of the burn house at the main door, firefighters supporting me with their hands on my shoulder so we wouldn't get separated in the dark. We entered the house, and the heat became intense. We rounded the corner where the fire was ablaze. Red, orange, and yellow flames crept up the walls—and it was hot! We knelt to get a better angle on the fire and unleashed the water, steam filling the small room. We worked the fire at different angles and varying levels. The lead trainer showed me how to work the fire hose most effectively. There was a lot more to it than I realized. And then, just like that, the fire was out.

We exited the burn house the same way we came in. Cool air greeted me as we pushed the door open. I was on an adrenaline high and exhausted at the same time. I was drenched in sweat, and that was only after 15 minutes. Exposing my ego and trying something new in front of my team gave me a greater understanding of what they do, and it also connected me with them. I had to put my trust in them, even though I felt completely vulnerable in that burn house. Watching them in their element and being a small part of their team gave me confidence in their abilities. My firefighters were truly experts in their field, and I would have to trust their decisions. This was a reminder to me that we need to have confidence in our subordinates and trust their judgment even in difficult circumstances.

Of course, my firefighters weren't looking for me to go out and fight the next fire, but they knew I was willing to listen and learn from them. I was able to show them I valued their expertise by putting my trust in their

Figure 10.2   With the firefighters from the 612th Air Base Squadron at Soto Cano Air Base in Honduras.

skills. Vulnerable leadership can be challenging, even intimidating, but it can also be exceptionally rewarding when we connect with our team.

Visiting with my team on their turf was one way to build relationships and connections, but I also tried to ensure I got the opportunity to get to know my team in social settings as well. It was another opportunity for me to get to know them, learn about their families and their goals in life. In each country I visited, I intentionally visited local restaurants with my team, tried new food like ceviche, pupusas, fried fish (with the head and tail included), and any other local delicacy my team recommended. I enjoyed the off-duty time with them, when we got the opportunity to share stories and experiences. Building relationships and connections was critical and helped us create an environment of trust.

YOU ARE THE EXPERTS. TEACH ME.

Every time I visited my geographically separated squadrons, I would spend a few days just visiting each of the sections to get some time to talk with my team. I found they were much more open with me and asked more questions in the smaller group setting, as opposed to a formal commander's call, where they were often afraid to ask questions. So, I would spend time walking around, seeing what they do, and visiting with them in their workspaces. By doing this, I more fully understood how I could advocate for them and what they needed from me to do their best work.

Over time, my team felt safe sharing their concerns as well as innovative ideas to get things done and ways to improve. I found that some of the most creative ideas came from the lower levels of my organization because they were often closest to the problem. And we won't find out about these ideas unless we engage with our teammates. I intentionally took the time to make them feel comfortable and asked them what they thought about specific problems or issues. But for this to be effective, I had to create an environment of trust by being vulnerable, connecting with my team, and showing the human side of leadership.

One of my squadrons was located at Naval Station Guantanamo Bay where they supported Joint Task Force Guantanamo's mission to conduct safe, humane, and legal detention operations. After landing at the airfield, we took a boat across the bay to the main side of the base. Once again, I checked into lodging, did a quick uniform change, then went out to meet with my team. My squadron primarily consisted of civil engineers who worked on the detention facilities. I was visiting with the heavy equipment team, also known as "dirt boys," when they asked if I wanted to learn how to drive a front loader. Learning from my experience with the firefighters at Soto Cano, I agreed to try it out. But again, there was a part of me that didn't want to make a mistake or do something stupid because I knew everyone was going to be watching. They pulled out the front loader, moved it into an undeveloped area where I couldn't do too much damage, and put me in the seat. The youngest airman in the group hopped up the ladder and began teaching me how to use the front bucket and how to move forward and backward over the mounds of dirt. It was a lot of fun until the tire popped, and we had to stop. Of course, that gave me another opportunity to get out and watch my vehicle maintenance technician change a tire. Apparently, changing a high-pressure tire is a bit more dangerous than driving the front loader, so it was something I could only watch him do while he talked me through the complicated process. It was important for me to see the work my team did and to understand the difficulty involved.

CONSIDERATIONS FOR LEADERS

When I look back on my time in command, the lessons learned from my airmen were some of the most memorable. I enjoyed learning from them and allowing them to show me their area of expertise. Yes, it was often uncomfortable because I was doing something I may not have been good at (and I wasn't in most cases) in front of my airmen. But they greatly appreciated my willingness to try, to experience what they do, and to see how they are experts in their field. I was always impressed with their ability to teach me, to break it down in a way I could understand. And in these moments, I built deeper connections with my team. So, how can you earn trust by showing the human side of leadership?

- Be open to uncertainty and risk. Create trust through vulnerability.
- Take the time to build relationships and connect with your team.
- Set your ego aside. Be willing to listen and learn from your team.

Showing the human side of leadership isn't easy, and in full transparency it still makes me uncomfortable to be open like this. But I've also learned we earn trust and build connections by being vulnerable, by taking risks, and by being open to new ideas and opportunities. *If you want to lead with courage, then show the human side of leadership. Take the time to build connections with your team.*

Chapter 11

CREATE YOUR OWN FLIGHT PLAN

"It is a mistake to look too far ahead. Only one link in the chain of destiny can be handled at a time."

—Winston S. Churchill

Figure 11.1 Our wedding on September 18, 1999, with all of the Air Force Academy graduates in attendance. We represented classes from 1970 to 1997.

CHOOSING YOUR OWN PATH

I received a lot of advice during my career about what was expected of me or what assignments would be best for my career. Most of the time though, the root of the advice centered on the idea that my husband (also an A-10 pilot) and I couldn't *both* be successful. It was made clear that we should expect to choose one career over another.

The best advice came from my commissioning officer when I graduated from the Air Force Academy: *In examining your life [in 10–20 years] may contentment and peace fill your heart in knowing you were on the "right path." Please remember, Kim, no one can tell you what that "path" is for you. Only you can choose the path that is right for you!*

I have leaned on those words throughout my career. Nobody lives your life but you, so only you can choose the path that is right for you. My husband and I decided that although we appreciated the advice and

153

care for our careers, we disagreed with choosing one career over another. We would continue doing what we loved until we decided it was time to do something else. We chose our own path.

MAKING IT WORK

Scott and I got married on September 18, 1999, after I finished graduate school and before I started pilot training. We had just enough time for a wedding and a honeymoon. Our friends like to point out this is also the Air Force's birthday, but we didn't plan that; it is mere coincidence. Our wedding was a fun mix of high school friends and Academy classmates. My closest friends from the Academy (Wendy, Tara, Shannon, and Beth), as well as my best friend from high school, Amy, served as my bridesmaids. Scott and I were excited about our new life together but knew there would be challenges along the way as well. During our first four years of marriage, we would spend only six months living together due to different assignments and multiple deployments.

Life as a dual military couple can be demanding. Many couples feel like they have to choose one career over the other, or both partners will leave the military because they have been unable to get assignments together. As an Air Force, we have done a better job in recent years in understanding this problem and finding ways to keep families together instead of separating married couples. According to the 2020 demographics profile published by the Department of Defense, 6.8% of active duty members are in dual-military marriages. The Air Force has the greatest percentage at 10.9%.[1] However, keeping a married couple together is not always possible due to rank, career field, or the needs of the Air Force. At the same time, the Air Force has also learned they are more likely to retain airmen when they keep families together.

It was tough for us to be apart during our first years of marriage, but we still made it work. When I was in pilot training at Columbus Air Force Base in Mississippi, Scott was stationed in North Carolina at Pope Air Force Base. We would meet in Atlanta every other weekend to spend time together. During our time apart, we learned some valuable lessons. We learned the importance of communication because if we didn't communicate well, we couldn't survive as a couple. We learned that trivial things could turn into big things if we didn't address them. We also learned that if we started looking too far ahead with assignment options, it would stress us out trying to figure out how to make it work. We learned to take it one assignment at a time. During those assignments, we realized our priorities or options could change, so it made sense not to look too far ahead. We thought about the goals we had for the future, but it made more sense to focus our time and effort on thinking about the next assignment versus the next five assignments. When we got the advice that we should choose one career over another, we decided to keep going in our careers as long as we both still enjoyed what we were doing. We each made sacrifices along the way, but we never chose one career over the other. Just as Major Schutzius reinforced to me at graduation, we had to choose the path that was right for us.

MUTUAL SUPPORT

When I deployed to Iraq in 2003, Scott was on the ground in Saudi Arabia running the air war to support Special Forces. He worked nights since most of the raids and activities occurred at night, so he was not awake when my April 7th mission occurred. After I landed and debriefed from that mission, I called and left a note with his intelligence officer to give me a call on a secure line when he got to work. Thankfully, he was oblivious to what had occurred until after I safely landed back in Kuwait. He woke up as usual on April 7th and walked over to the mission-planning cell. Along the way, he ran into his two-star general boss, who looked over at him and said very sincerely, "Soup [my husband's call sign], glad your wife is okay." Then, as he walked into the operations building, he was immediately surrounded by people asking how I was doing. He knew something was up. He walked to his desk and found a note that said, "Soup, your wife was hit over Baghdad. She's fine, she wants you to give her a call."

We would later talk about what happened over a secure line with about 20 people in the room listening to one side of the conversation. Because the line was secure (classified) I was able to share the entire story with him. We finally saw each other a few months later when he stopped by Kuwait on his way home so we could have a few short but much needed days together.

COMING HOME

I often felt mixed emotions coming home from a deployment. I was excited to see my family and friends, but I also felt like I was leaving something behind. We had committed so much of ourselves to the missions in Iraq and Afghanistan, to our brothers and sisters on the ground, and now we were home. We were no longer responsible for saving lives. We no longer spent our days reviewing intelligence reports for what was happening and coming up with new ways to adjust our mission. I watched the news, but it felt like the war was a world away now.

After deployment, we were granted two weeks of leave, time off to decompress and let it all go. But it was hard to walk away. It wasn't like a light switch that you could just shut off. We had confidence in the next team, but in some ways we still wanted to be there, to do our part. To be fair, part of me was irritated knowing that so few Americans were paying attention to what was happening in Afghanistan or Iraq. Our military was still in the fight, and yet, at home, most people weren't even paying attention. In general, everyone was supportive of the military, but they just didn't see what was happening every day in the war against terrorism, so they lost interest. It was a tough transition for me, and it took time to truly relax.

By the end of 2003, Scott and I had been on back-to-back deployments for more than a year and we had little time together as a family, even if it was just the two of us and our yellow lab, Scout. We had barely spent any time together in the first house we bought because the mission had come first. We took turns being home alone while the other deployed, and that continuous rotation had finally come to an end. Coming home from our deployments was an opportunity for us to start again.

We needed to disconnect from the realities of life and just spend time together. So, we took some time to get away to the mountains in Gatlinburg, Tennessee. On one of our long bus rides to kayak the Pigeon River, we finally started talking about our combat experiences, not just what we did, but how we felt about it. I talked about being afraid on that long flight home from Baghdad. I was worried I could have died without doing all the things I wanted to do in life. We talked about what was important to us, what really mattered. I finally admitted to someone, my husband, how scared I was on that April 7th mission. I had experienced a life-changing moment, one in which I wasn't sure I was going to survive, but I was determined to learn from it and help others learn from my experience.

Finally talking about all of it—my fears, my stress, my anxiety in that moment—gave me focus and a way to move forward. I would focus my life on what mattered, and I would share my story with others so they could learn from my experience, too.

NICKELS ON THE GRASS

Fighter pilots know there is risk in what we do. Every mission has risks. We brief those risks, talk about how to mitigate them, and then we move on. Some missions involve more risks than others . . . low altitude, night operations, weather, and night vision goggles (NVGs) use to name a few. And sometimes, we combine those mission elements, increasing the risk.

Flying with NVGs can be inherently dangerous but necessary because many of the missions in Afghanistan or Iraq were flown at night. NVGs can amplify available light, allowing you to see infrared light sources such as target designation lasers or strobes marking friendly positions, but they limit depth perception and eliminate peripheral vision. Despite what you see in the movies, NVGs don't turn night into day. It's like looking through a soda straw because the view is so limited, so a pilot can easily lose context with what is around them. In combat, it was critical to have a cross-check that reminded you to look outside underneath your goggles, inside at your flight instruments, and then back again through the NVG "soda straw." While there was risk flying with NVGs, there were benefits as well. They empowered us to be more efficient and effective in our support to ground troops at night. Therefore, units needed to spend time upgrading pilots to use NVGs before they deployed.

In 2004, one of our sister A-10 units, the 355th Fighter Squadron, stationed at Eielson Air Force Base in Alaska, was busy preparing for their rotation to Afghanistan. A good friend of ours, Captain Jonathan "Cosmo" Scheer, was the squadron's weapons officer and was responsible for ensuring his pilots were ready to deploy. On February 25, 2004, a four-ship of A-10s took off from Eielson Air Force Base on an NVG upgrade mission, training for NVG takeoffs and landings, a relatively new and particularly difficult skill. At 8:31 p.m., just two minutes after takeoff, one of those A-10s impacted the ground 3.5 miles north of the base.

As soon as we heard about the crash, my husband called Cosmo at work to make sure he was okay. The pilot on the other end of the phone couldn't hold back and broke down. He told my husband the terrible news. Cosmo wasn't okay. He was the pilot of the A-10 that had crashed. We were devastated. He was just at our house staying with us a week prior. We had just gone skiing together. This couldn't be true.

Based on evidence obtained during the accident investigation, the board president said he believed the accident was caused when Cosmo became spatially disoriented and was unable to gain situational awareness until it was too late to either recover the aircraft or safely eject. Weather conditions the night of the crash made it difficult to see the horizon, and other pilots said there was little or no horizon from which to reference the aircraft's attitude. Spatial disorientation can be debilitating and, in many cases, deadly.

After Cosmos's accident, we gathered in Colorado Springs at the Air Force Academy for his funeral. Scott wasn't there with me because, in his memorial instructions, Cosmo had asked my husband to lead the missing man formation. Even though fighter pilots think we are invincible, many of us have complete plans for what happens if we don't make it, where we will be buried, who will escort our body, and how we want the ceremony to happen. Deep down we all know it's a deadly business, and we prepare for the worst. We know that the business of flying fighters is fraught with extreme levels of risk, including death, and yet we do it anyway. We do our best to manage a sense of invincibility in the face of reality.

The Air Force Academy cemetery is stunning with green grass, pine trees, and the Rocky Mountains looming in the background. I have too many friends and classmates buried there. On this day, as we said goodbye to Cosmo, I was keenly aware of my other friends and classmates who were laid to rest nearby. Each shot of the 21-gun salute caused my body to shake. As the bugler played taps, we all kept our eyes on the sky overhead. We knew they were coming. As the last note of taps sounded, the A-10s roared overhead, with one A-10 pulling up high into the sky, leaving the formation. It was tough for all of us to keep it together. As we left the cemetery that day, we would pay our final respects to Cosmo by throwing a nickel on the grass near his grave, a tradition that dates back to the Korean War.

I would throw many nickels on the grass over the years. It was never easy, but this was the risk of flight. Cosmo's accident once again put life into perspective for us. We made sure we had plans in place if the worst happened to either of us. We talked about where we wanted to be buried, who would handle the details, and ensured our wills were up-to-date. It was a tough conversation, but one we had to have.

"TIMING" A FAMILY

After about 10 years of marriage, we decided it was time to start a family. With deployments right after 9/11 followed by busy assignments at the Weapons School and Test Squadron at Nellis Air Force Base, we just weren't ready to have kids at that time. So, we waited. In 2008, we received orders to go to Fort Leavenworth, Kansas, for the Army's Command and General Staff College (CGSC), a non-flying assignment. CGSC would meet the requirements for our intermediate developmental education, which was the professional military education (PME) required at the midpoint of an Air Force officer's career. PME is designed to educate and professionally broaden officers, helping us to start viewing issues at the operational and strategic level rather than a singular focus on day-to-day tactics.

We thought our upcoming assignment at CGSC would be the perfect time to start a family since I would not be on flying status while there. We were trying to time the pregnancy and birth to happen while I was at school so as not to affect my unit and flying capability. At the time, women flying fighter aircraft were grounded from flying as soon as they became pregnant. Medical personnel believed that the risk was too high in terms of flying a fighter aircraft susceptible to G-forces as well as the possibility of ejection. Rules have since changed and now all pregnant aircrew are authorized to apply for a waiver regardless of trimester, aircraft, or flight profile.[2] However, for me, as an A-10 pilot in 2008, I was grounded immediately. At the time, I had mixed emotions about the rules since I was still on flying status and assigned to a flying unit.

I found out I was pregnant close to the Christmas holidays, so I had some time to process everything and come up with a plan of how to tell my team. The first step was to break the news to my commander. I picked a day when there were very few people in the squadron since most were out on holiday leave. I stopped by my commander's office and asked if he had a few minutes to talk. I was nervous about what he would think. I felt like I was letting the squadron down since being pregnant would ground me from flying. I told him I was pregnant and apologized that it happened a little sooner than I expected. He looked at me with shock . . . shock that I was apologizing. He was ecstatic for me and my husband. He knew us both and was genuinely happy for us. I felt a huge sense of relief.

After informing my squadron commander, I gathered my team from the A-10 Division together and told them the news. Again, I was nervous about what they would think. The reality was, they were ecstatic, too. Why did I ever think they would be disappointed? I was worried that by being pregnant, I would be letting my team down because I couldn't do my part. I was hired to be a pilot, and a pilot should be flying with the unit. But these were my brothers, and they were genuinely happy for us. I took on all the non-flying duties that no pilot liked to do anyway so it allowed my team to fly more frequently.

This was a poignant moment for me, sharing something so personal with my team. I was so worried about what they would think of me as a leader that I failed to realize how happy they would be for me as a person. Why did I separate the two? I was slowly learning that it was okay to be human (and a woman). It was okay to have a life outside of the Air Force and okay to be vulnerable with my team. I didn't always have to be a tough, fearless fighter pilot. I had to stop putting additional pressure on myself that didn't exist.

ONE FINAL DEPLOYMENT

After a year at Command and General Staff College, Scott and I found ourselves back at Davis-Monthan Air Force Base again, but this time on track to become leaders in the Fighter Group. We were at the peak of our careers in the A-10 community and combat-proven fighter pilots, but we were also new parents trying to figure out how to do it all.

After a short time at Davis-Monthan, I got a surprise deployment order from Headquarters Air Force. The requirement was to deploy a close air support expert to Kabul for 180 days to augment work at ISAF (International Security Assistance Force) Joint Command. Even though I had already deployed several times, I fit the requirements for this deployment and was selected to deploy as an individual augmentee. I would be working at ISAF Joint Command (IJC) headquarters located at Kabul International Airport running air operations for ISAF. Headquarters IJC, the three-star NATO joint war-fighting command in Afghanistan, was one of several major subordinate commands to Headquarters ISAF. Established in November 2009, the command allows ISAF to focus on "up and out" (strategic issues) while IJC controls the "down and in" (operational fight).[3]

I have to admit, this was the first time I was less than excited to deploy. My husband had just taken command of a squadron and our son, Colin, was only a year old. When the notification became official, I had to quick-turn to my pre-deployment training in Stavanger, Norway. I had about a week to prepare so it was a tough time for us, and we called on our family to help. They supported us multiple times throughout this deployment, and we really couldn't have done it without them.

I was at a low point in my Air Force career. I didn't want to leave my son at home, and I vowed I would get out of the Air Force as soon as I returned from deployment. I just couldn't fathom spending any more time away from my young son. I jokingly told my husband before I left that all I needed him to do as a single parent was to make sure Colin didn't break any bones and that I didn't come home to a two-year-old dropping the "F-bomb."

At the time of my deployment in 2010, American and NATO forces were on track to suffer the deadliest year ever in Afghanistan since the Taliban was overthrown in late 2001. Troop numbers also peaked in 2010 due to the surge in forces directed by the Obama administration, with numbers totaling around 100,000 forces on the ground. Pentagon figures reflected the growing violence in Afghanistan as more troops arrived and the Taliban increased the number of its attacks against coalition forces.[4]

I arrived in Kabul, exhausted and miserable for the first month. I was not flying, and I didn't want to be there. Being a staff officer is tough for operators. Most of the time, we viewed the staff as people who get in the way of doing the job. I certainly didn't feel the camaraderie I usually did when I had deployed with a unit. It was a completely different experience being on the ground in Kabul and not being part of a flying squadron. I immediately missed feeling like I was part of a team. I didn't know anyone. I worked and slept, and that was about it. I was lonely and miserable thinking about the family that I had left behind. After a few weeks, I got into a routine and settled into the deployment. I finally felt like what I was doing was at least worthwhile and making a difference in the war on terrorism. It made it easier to be apart from my family, although I still missed them immensely.

Despite the impressive technology we have today to communicate with friends and family overseas, communication between the United States and Kabul was sketchy at best back then. Skype was the best option, but our internet capability was unbelievably poor at the time. I would wander around the base with my laptop searching for the best signal. Oftentimes, this meant sitting outside on the dusty ground, trying not to move, just so I could complete a Skype call. I felt like I was missing out on so much of my son's early life. I was afraid he wouldn't remember me when I got home. During my six-month deployment, I just wanted to see my son and watch him grow up. He had other plans of course. He wasn't overly interested in talking to me on the computer, especially with a blurry or grainy picture where it was hard to even discern who you were talking to. He thought it was more fun to shut the laptop screen while we were talking, which of course ended the call.

Colin turned two years old while I was in Kabul, and it was agonizing for me to miss his birthday party. We planned it so I could watch via Skype, but I still felt like an outsider at my own son's party. My friends Casey and Andra were there with their kids, and they were all trying to make me feel part of the celebration. It was heartbreaking not to be there, but I was also thankful for the support of our friends and neighbors who helped us get through a very challenging time. I kept a brave face during the party watching him eat cake and open presents, but when it was done, I closed my laptop and cried. Once again, I was struggling to decide if this was worth it.

My job in Kabul was the deputy commander for the air operations center for ISAF Joint Command, responsible for theater-wide management of all air operations in support of Operation Enduring Freedom. As the deputy, I led the night shift for six months. I would monitor all air operations at night, review all kinetic activities, and advise the senior ISAF leadership at the morning meeting regarding any event of interest. If we put bombs on any structure, then that was a reportable incident. If there was any potential for civilian casualties, then that was the wake-up criteria for my boss, who happened to be a two-star German officer. The headquarters building was full of our international partners as well as sister services. It was a unique experience and, looking back, I am thankful for the opportunity to have served alongside them. During my time at IJC, I helped coordinate 132 close air support events in support of elections in Afghanistan. I also helped guide 12 personnel recovery operations, coordinating efforts with multiple theater-level agencies. In the end, we were able to help recover 64 military and civilian personnel.

Finally, after six months of working 12-hour night shifts, I reached the end of my deployment. I was anxious to get home to see my family but worried that my son wouldn't remember me. When I came down the stairs at Tucson International Airport, I only saw my husband at first. My son was hiding behind his legs, peeking out at me. He remembered me, but he was still shy. I sat with him in the back seat on the way home and by the time we finished the 20-minute drive home, he wouldn't leave my side. Colin is now 14 years old and doesn't remember me being gone at all.

Despite my confidence that this would be the end of my Air Force career, I decided to stay in the Air Force and serve another 11 years after my deployment. As soon as I got home from my deployment, I became the director of operations for the 357th Fighter Squadron. I would be back flying the A-10 full-time and working with our newest generation of A-10 pilots. I couldn't turn that down. I wanted to be part of training the pilots who would follow me. I had a lot to share, and I was committed to teaching and improving the next generation. And so, I stayed when I had planned to leave, which would become a repeat occurrence throughout my career.

STRIVING FOR WORK–LIFE BALANCE

After a brief stint as the director of operations, I was selected for squadron command. Scott and I would be squadron commanders at the same time. He was in command of the 358th Fighter Squadron while I commanded the 355th Operations Support Squadron. We regularly sat in meetings together with both the group and wing commander, and my squadron would support his squadron in terms of weather, intelligence briefings, and aircrew flight equipment. We worked together well and understood what we each were dealing with. Our schedules were sometimes difficult, trying to deconflict early or late flights that interfered with our son's pickup time at the child development center on base, but we managed to make it work. There would be nights when we were both working on officer/enlisted performance reports or promotion recommendation forms that we just didn't have time to finish during the workday. We would come home from work, play with our son, have dinner, do our bedtime routine, and then get to work on our laptops to finish what we could not do during the normal workday. Because we had such similar careers, we truly were a support network for one another. He was my wingman at home whom I could count on to support me but also to give me honest feedback. I did the same for him. We managed day-to-day life through a true partnership in which we were committed to having each other's backs, supporting each other, and sharing in each other's successes and failures.

Scott's time in command was coming to an end, and by Air Force time-lines he was scheduled to go to school for his next assignment to complete senior developmental education or SDE. I still had to finish squadron command, so we were preparing to spend another year apart. We asked to get Scott's school delayed, but the Air Force didn't want to slow him down. So, we asked for an early release from command so I could go to Washington, DC, with Scott. I was now pregnant with baby number two, so we wanted to be together. It didn't look like that was going to happen, so we started discussing how we could make it work. We discussed Scott taking our oldest son with him to DC and I would stay at Davis-Monthan, where we had a good support network to finish out squadron command with a newborn baby. I knew it would be tough, but we would make it work. Then, unexpectedly, I received notification of a pending assign-ment. It came directly to my inbox as an automated email. I ignored it for most of the day because it just appeared to be an automated message from the Air Force Personnel Center that was not time sensitive. I sat there in shock when I opened it and saw the message. Somewhere, someone had decided that it was important to keep us together and approved my move to DC. I had avoided a Pentagon staff tour up to this point, but it was finally my turn to serve on the staff at the Pentagon. Most fighter pilots try to avoid Pentagon staff assignments (because it's staff work and not tacti-cal), but it would be worth it if it meant Scott and I could stay together as we welcomed our second child.

After a year at the Pentagon, I was selected to go to school for my SDE. I would take a nontraditional approach and spend my one year allocated for SDE working at the Atlantic Council as the Air Force Senior Fellow. The Atlantic Council is a nonpartisan organization that aims to stimulate US leadership and engagement in the world, in partnership with allies and partners, to shape solutions to global challenges. My time at the At-lantic Council was a unique opportunity to see how things worked in DC. I wore suits and heels to work in place of my flight suit and combat boots. I also enjoyed getting out in DC, visiting different think tanks and expand-ing my views. I appreciated the opportunity to work with visiting fellows to learn different perspectives. It was a pleasant change of pace from the high-paced operations tempo I had experienced throughout my career. It also happened to be perfect timing since Scott was selected for group command in Afghanistan on a one-year deployment.

THE STRUGGLE TO DO IT ALL

When my husband deployed to Afghanistan for a year, being the mom at home was one of the most challenging roles I've ever experienced. My boys were just one and five years old at the time. The youngest didn't understand it all, but it was exceptionally hard on my five-year-old who missed his dad immensely. We tried to do all the things recommended for deployed families. We had Daddy Dolls made for the kids, a small doll with a picture of my husband on it, and a recorded message inside the doll that the kids could hear when they pushed a button. I always thought it was strange at night when I heard my husband's voice over the baby monitor before I realized the kids were pushing the button or had rolled over on the doll in their sleep.

I had done my own deployments to Iraq and Afghanistan, but this was different and, frankly, harder in many ways. Now, I was the one at home, doing my best to raise two kids while also working a full-time job in the Air Force. I was trying to be a mom, fighter pilot, wife, and leader all at the same time. The struggle to do it all was real!

To be honest, there were many days I didn't feel like I was doing any of those jobs well. I quickly realized I couldn't do it alone. But it took me time to figure out how to ask for help. Thankfully, my friends, family, and neighbors were more than willing to help. I just had to be brave enough to ask. The saying "it takes a village" was in full force during that deployment. I couldn't have made it through that year, especially the holidays, without the help of so many people. We hired a babysitter to help me with the kids after school. We had family visit us for weeks at a time. Our church family and neighbors made meals and helped with the kids. Being at home during Scott's deployment gave me greater admiration for our military spouses who deal with deployments repeatedly. They have my utmost respect for holding down the fort while their spouses are away. The experience also gave me a way to connect with the spouses of my airmen because I genuinely understood what they were going through.

That deployment reinforced to me that there's no shame in asking for help when we need it. Even leaders, especially leaders, need to ensure we have a support network. We don't have to do it alone. A robust support network both in our personal and professional lives can truly make a difference. *Do I need help at home with things like groceries or cleaning (my least favorite chores) so I can focus on the most important things? Do I need*

Figure 11.2 Welcoming Scott home after a one-year deployment to Afghanistan. There was so much relief and joy in that moment.

the help of an executive coach or mentor at work who can talk me through the challenges I'm facing? It takes courage to be vulnerable, to admit we can't do it all on our own, and to ask for help. But strong, courageous leaders know when it's time to ask for help. I was a better mom, fighter pilot, wife, and leader because of it.

A FEMALE ROLE MODEL

As my time at the Atlantic Council came to an end, I knew the Air Force would be looking for a new job for me that would fill my joint require-ment. To progress through the ranks, military officers are required to spend 36 months in a joint assignment where they work with officers from other military services. I was selected for promotion to colonel so I knew this job would be challenging in a new way. I got a phone call from the Colonels Group, the Air Force organization responsible for all colonel as-signments, about an interview for the position of Military Assistant to the Undersecretary of Defense for Policy or USDP.

The incoming Undersecretary of Defense for Policy was Ms. Christine Wormuth. USDP is the number three in the Office of the Secretary of

Defense, only behind the Secretary of Defense and the Deputy Secretary of Defense when it comes to policy issues. As USDP, she would advise the Secretary of Defense on the full range of regional and functional national security issues. She would also frequently represent the Department of Defense (DoD) at the White House and would spend considerable time on the counter-ISIS campaign, the rebalance to Asia, counterterrorism operations, and US defense relations with countries in Europe, Asia, and the Middle East. I knew the job would entail long hours and a lot of traveling, so I planned to go into the interview and politely decline the opportunity. I didn't see a way I could do the job with two kids under the age of six at home and a husband who wouldn't return from Afghanistan for three more months.

After answering questions and sharing some of my experiences in the interview, I quickly realized I respected Ms. Wormuth and connected with her beliefs and values. She was a strong professional who had worked her way up in the ranks with two kids of her own at home. I explained my concerns to her, and she was confident we could make it work. I was shocked. I had wanted to say no, but here was a senior DoD official willing to work within my constraints. She genuinely understood my challenges and she still wanted me for the job. I knew I could excel in this environment and was now excited for the opportunity. I walked out of the interview, called my parents and my husband, and told them I wanted to take the job if it was offered to me. We worked together to come up with a plan to help me survive while my husband was deployed, which of course involved my family traveling to DC to help once again. With their help, I felt comfortable I could handle it, so I wrote Ms. Wormuth to let her know I had a plan and wanted the job. A few days later, I got the call and accepted the job as military assistant to USDP.

Working in the Pentagon in the Office of the Secretary of Defense was an amazing opportunity. For the first time in my military career, I was operating at the strategic level. Ms. Wormuth allowed me to sit in on high-level meetings, and she regularly asked my opinion about key military issues. I learned the significance of feeling valued for what you do. I was always willing to work hard because I knew what I did made a difference. The hours were sometimes long, but she was always understanding if I had to leave early. It was an exciting and rewarding job, but after two years at the Pentagon, I was eager to get back to the operational community.

TAKING ITS TOLL

As we looked at possible follow-on assignments, we struggled with figuring out how we could stay together. We now had two children and we couldn't fathom separating us or them. So, we decided we would do whatever it took to stay together. My husband was eligible for Wing Command, and I was eligible for Group Command. However, since we were married, I couldn't work for my husband in his chain of command. According to Air Force rules, it would be a conflict of interest if my husband was my supervisor. And it might not have been that great for life at home either. There were few options available where we could stay together, but we reinforced to the Colonels Group that this was our priority. Eventually, with help from senior leadership, we were both assigned to Davis-Monthan Air Force Base in Tucson, Arizona, where my husband would take command of the 355th Fighter Wing and I would take command of the 612th Theater Operations Group and 474th Air Expeditionary Group.

Since most of my airmen were overseas in deployed locations, I spent about two to three weeks each month on the road visiting with them. It was tough being gone that much as we now had a four-year-old and an eight-year-old; leaving every other week was difficult for all of us. It was important for me to check on the morale and welfare of my airmen, but I was also concerned about my kids. I wasn't home as much as I needed or wanted to be, and my husband was extremely busy as the Wing Commander, responsible for more than 11,000 airmen on the installation. We couldn't get through this time without help, and so we once again relied on family, friends, and a babysitter to help us with the kids after school. It was one of the most challenging times of our career with two time-intensive positions, but we powered through and made it work. I found myself once again navigating personal and professional challenges. Despite the struggle of leaving my kids at home, I loved visiting with my airmen and learning about their missions. I got energy from them and always came away excited about my role as their commander.

Although I enjoyed my job as a Group Commander, the time away from home was difficult for my family. My husband also had TDYs (temporary duty) about one week each month for promotion boards or wing commander meetings. We tried to deconflict our schedules so that one of us was always home with the kids. But it still took its toll on our family. Our oldest son, Colin, was mostly angry about our travel and time away.

He didn't like when Scott would come home from work and then have to go out for an evening event. On one occasion, Colin even told our three-star boss that he wished we would get fired because he didn't like our jobs. Our youngest son, Brodie, who was four at the time, asked me one night, "When are we going to be a family again?" Talk about a knife through the heart. We loved what we were doing, but we knew it was time to take a break for our kids. They needed more time with us, and we needed more time as a family.

Unfortunately, taking a time-out doesn't fit with standard Air Force career progression. My husband and I were both promoted below the zone (two years early) to Lieutenant Colonel and Colonel, so taking some downtime wasn't really in the standard playbook. Based on policies at the time, the Air Force required me to compete for Wing Command or submit my retirement paperwork. My husband was up for another staff assignment after his Wing Command tour and according to the Colonels Group, there were limited options for us to stay together. I wasn't ready to retire, but I just couldn't fathom taking on Wing Command after the past two years of Group and Wing Command combined for our family. After many long nights of deliberation, I decided it would be best to retire from the Air Force. My husband made the same decision. And so, I reluctantly submitted my retirement paperwork. This wasn't a popular decision, but we had to choose the path that was right for our family.

The decision to stay on and serve or retire is a difficult one for many military members. This was something I had committed my life to for 20 years. I wasn't quite ready to hang it all up, but at the same time, I knew I had to make some changes for my family. After everything was said and done, I wanted to ensure my family was by my side.

FINDING BALANCE

According to a study conducted by RAND, in the Air Force, female officers currently make up 21.1% of officers in the rank of second lieutenant through lieutenant colonel, but only 13.9% of officers at the colonel level, and only 7.5% of officers at brigadier general or higher.[5] The study goes on to say that one factor contributing to this underrepresentation is that women tend to leave the active duty Air Force at higher rates than men. In the RAND study, female Air Force officer focus groups discussed children or the desire to have a family as major factors influencing decisions to remain in or leave the service, noting the difficulty of frequent moves, deployments, and demanding work schedules. I struggled with these issues myself, and as I progressed in rank and the demands on my time increased, I felt pulled in many different directions.

I've had plenty of challenges trying to achieve a balance between my personal and professional life. But I've found that we can achieve work–life balance if we don't think it has to be a 50–50 balance every day. Some days, work demands my attention, and I may stay later than normal or do work at home, but on other days, I may leave work early to spend time with my kids. Trying to do it all and have a 50–50 balance every day just isn't realistic. We need to give ourselves some grace when it comes to work–life balance. Sometimes that balance comes over a week, or a month, or maybe even a year. Whatever it is for you, give yourself some grace and know it's not always going to work out as planned.

Leaders have a responsibility to set the example and create a culture where work–life balance is a priority. We need to walk the walk and show our team that we can do it, too. It's not good enough to just say it's a priority, then be the first one in and the last one out of the office. If we make the effort to find an overall balance between our personal and professional life, our team will follow our lead. When we feel we have achieved that balance (or are at least working toward it), then we will be more productive and more satisfied.

CONSIDERATIONS FOR LEADERS

You will get plenty of input and advice about your life and career. *What do you want? What's most important to you? How do you define success?* To create your own flight plan it is important to do the following:

- Choose a path that brings you fulfillment. If your current path does not, then choose another.
- Make deliberate choices about which opportunities to pursue and which to decline.
- Use caution in planning too far ahead. Focus on the immediate timeline of what you can control while also keeping sight of long term goals and dreams.

- Prioritize what is most important to you. *Where are you willing to make sacrifices?*
- Give yourself some grace when things don't go as planned. Avoid putting too much pressure on yourself.

As I've mentored and coached young leaders throughout the years, I have imparted this advice as well. Make decisions for you and your family that are right for you based on the path you have chosen. You cannot please everyone. Set your priorities and choose the path that is right for you, not the path someone else thinks you should take. Write your own story. **If you want to lead with courage, then create your own flight plan. Only you can choose the path that is right for you.**

Chapter 12

COMMANDER'S INTENT

"Acting without orders, in anticipation of orders, or without waiting for approval must become second nature in any form of warfare where formations do not fight closely en cadre, and must go down to the smallest units. It requires in the higher command a corresponding flexibility of mind, confidence in its subordinates, and the power to make its intentions clear right through the force."
—Field-Marshal Viscount Slim, Commander, British Army

Figure 12.1 My change of command ceremony, relinquishing command of the 612th Theater Operations Group and 474th Air Expeditionary Group at Davis-Monthan Air Force Base in Arizona. Photo credit: Staff Sergeant Danny Rangel.

Military joint doctrine describes the commander's intent as the clear and concise expression of what the force must do and the conditions the force must establish to accomplish the mission. It includes the purpose, end state, and associated risks. The purpose of a commander's intent is to allow subordinates the greatest possible freedom of action. It provides focus to the team and helps subordinate commanders act to achieve the commander's objectives in absence of further orders especially when the operation does not unfold as planned. Successful commanders demand subordinate leaders at all levels exercise disciplined initiative and act aggressively and independently to accomplish the mission within the commander's intent. A well-crafted commander's intent improves the team's situational awareness, which enables timely and effective actions in fluid, chaotic situations.

COMMANDER'S INTENT IN ACTION

Before launching on a combat mission in Iraq or Afghanistan, we would get updates on the ground commander's intent to ensure we understood what was happening on the ground. In Iraq, this meant stopping by the Operations Center to get a briefing from our ground liaison officer, or GLO, an Army officer assigned to Air Force units to help translate Army scheme of maneuver and activity to Air Force personnel. Our GLO would provide us updates on ground activity and relay the ground commander's intent. We needed to have a clear understanding so we could make accurate tactical-level decisions that supported the larger strategic objectives. To make it simple, tell me what to do and why, then it's my job as an A-10 pilot to figure out how to accomplish it. We were experts in the close air support role, and we knew how to best provide the support that our ground troops so desperately needed. World War II Army General George Patton stated it this way: "Never tell people how to do things, tell them what to do and they will surprise you with their ingenuity."

Sometimes, we would show up to support an isolated ground unit, and they would be lacking the bigger picture. One afternoon, we showed up overhead after receiving a call for close air support.

"Hog 1, we have enemy working on the east side of the bridge, request bombs on that position."

"Negative," my flight lead responded quickly. "There are too many civilians in the area, and we have guidance not to destroy key infrastructure."

We questioned the choice of weapons because we knew the bridge was intended to be used later by our friendly forces. We knew this because we understood the larger ground scheme of maneuver and the commander's intent of maintaining key lines of communication (in this case, bridges and roadways that would later be used by friendly forces). If we dropped bombs on the bridge, it would be destroyed, causing significant delays for our forces. Instead of using bombs on the bridge, we elected to use guns and rockets on the enemy location so we could be more accurate and not cause considerable damage to the bridge structure itself. We just needed to know what effects they needed, and we could determine the best weapons to use. Because we understood the ground commander's intent, we were better prepared to make time-critical decisions while supporting the mission.

In Afghanistan, we had a similar routine, but it was often more critical to get that information before we launched because once we were airborne and deep into the Hindu Kush Mountain ranges, we could often lose communication with any other outside controlling agencies. We had to be clear on the commander's intent so we could make time-critical decisions without having to call back to ask for permission or seek clarification.

One of our primary roles at Bagram Air Base was to sit alert to respond to a call for close air support. We had to be ready to launch within minutes on an unknown mission in an unknown location. Since we rarely knew exactly what we were going to be doing on a mission, we had to be clear on the commander's intent before launching. One afternoon while sitting alert, we received word that our two-ship of A-10s needed to launch as quickly as possible. We hurried out to the jets, got our gear on, started the engines, and received our tasking. Our mission was to look for a red truck coming from the eastern side of Afghanistan that intelligence relayed was carrying a vehicle-borne improvised explosive device or VBIED. We launched and proceeded immediately to the eastern border of Afghanistan. We spent hours scouring the roads coming in from Pakistan, trying to find a red truck. It was like finding a needle in a haystack. There were endless numbers of roads coming into Afghanistan and we tried to closely search them all. We had the approval to fly low so we could visually identify anything suspicious in the back of the pickup trucks. We also had the approval to destroy the truck if we found it. We would likely have to make a split-second decision; there would be no time to ask permission.

Finally, after several hours of searching, there it was . . . a lone red truck moving slowly through the mountainside pass. It looked like this could be the truck as the back end was covered with what appeared to be a tarp and metal coming out of the sides. I decided to do one low pass to get a closer look and be immediately ready to follow up with a gun pass on the truck. I quickly pointed my nose at the ground, diving behind the truck while trying to get a closer look. My wingman was high overhead monitoring the situation and ready to roll in with guns if needed. As I crossed the back of the truck, the tarp flew up, and it became immediately apparent that the back of the truck was filled with goats in cages, not explosives . . . no VBIED to be found. Thankfully, we had clear guidance. Find the red truck, take it out, but do not risk civilian casualties if we couldn't positively identify the truck. Our commanders trusted us to make the right

Figure 12.2　After landing from my final combat mission. That American flag was with me on every combat mission, from Iraq to Afghanistan.

call because we understood their intent. They weren't monitoring our every action; they trusted us to execute the mission and use our judgment if the situation was unclear.

INTENT PROVIDES EMPOWERMENT

In 2016, as commander of the 612th Theater Operations Group and the 474th Air Expeditionary Group, my airmen were dispersed in various locations overseas conducting a wide variety of missions. My team of squadron commanders (my direct reports) were deployed throughout the region and responsible for their team and mission sets. As the group commander (think CEO), I needed to have oversight and awareness of operations without being overly involved in the day-to-day details. I needed to trust my subordinate commanders to know their job and do it well. I also expected them to up-channel information to me so I could have the bigger picture and spend time thinking about the strategic view instead of over-controlling the daily tactical details. Additionally, I needed to know when my team needed help, advice, or assistance.

When I first met with my subordinate commanders, I gave them my commander's intent and ensured they understood both what to do in terms of the mission and why we were doing it. I needed to be confident that they understood so they could in turn relay and explain that information to their teams. I wanted to empower my subordinate commanders to lead their teams, make their own decisions based on solid planning and preparation, and lead with courage. They needed to feel confident in what they were doing and why. I trusted them to do their jobs well and align with my commander's intent. I expected them to execute, ask for help when they needed it, keep me updated on operations, and ensure I was informed when there were issues that needed my attention. I wanted them to feel empowered to do their jobs, but also know that I would have their backs. If they could effectively focus on the tactical level operations, then I could focus on the bigger picture. I monitored their progress and knew when it was time to intervene. I didn't expect them to be perfect or have all the answers, so I provided mentoring and feedback as needed along the way.

Our team members must understand the *what* and *why* of our mission. The *how* can then be left up to them. When subordinate commanders and leaders understand the intent and the purpose behind an order or decision, then they can take the initiative to act in critical moments without asking permission, thereby seizing fleeting opportunities.

DRIVING CHANGE BY SHARING INTENT

As a new leader, and in the first few months of command, I would always spend time learning and listening. After meeting with my team, watching firsthand what they were doing, and listening to their ideas and concerns, I began to develop a new way forward for some of our policies and procedures. Not everyone liked the new policies and plans at first. It was different from the way we had always done things, and it required some members of my team to change the way they had been doing business. Several of my airmen had been in the region a lot longer than I had, had more experience in the region, and were used to doing things a certain way. It turns out that "we've always done it this way" is not synonymous with the most effective or efficient way.

One of my forward operating locations (FOLs) was on the island of Curaçao. Most people know Curaçao as a tourist destination and a stop for cruise ships, but it was also a crucial location to support counterdrug operations in the region. Our team was responsible for the FOL, and we had security forces personnel assigned to secure the FOL for aircraft that passed through or deployed to Curaçao to support the counterdrug mission. There were a few aircraft that required additional security, and so we maintained a higher number of security forces personnel to meet that demand. However, on a day-to-day basis when those aircraft weren't at the FOL, we had more people than were needed. Nobody ever wants to give up personnel, but I knew there was a demand for security forces personnel overseas in places like Iraq and Afghanistan. I asked a lot of questions about our security posture and why we continued to keep the higher number of personnel. Most of the answers fell along the lines of "We've had that number since the FOL opened, and we've always done it this way."

I continued to ask questions and seek out experts who were more knowledgeable about security operations and manning. I talked to our team and asked where we could find creative solutions. If we drew down our numbers, then when those aircraft arrived, it would mean our team would have to work longer hours or that some of our leaders would be required out on the flight line. At the time, these aircraft were only making one to two trips to the FOL per year (averaging about three weeks on the ground), so it seemed like a reasonable approach to draw down our staffing to ensure we weren't pulling from other higher priority missions. But this was a change, and naturally not everyone liked it. I understood that it put more pressure on my team in the short term, but it also took the pressure off the entire security forces community in the long term. As I walked through my decision with the team, explaining the reasoning, and the *why* behind my decision, people started to understand and could see why it wasn't only about our team in Curaçao. Rather, we had to look at the bigger picture. In general, people don't like change because they are comfortable with the status quo, and they often fear the unknown. To help with that, I made every effort to listen to my team's concerns and ideas before making significant changes because they often had information and expertise needed in the decision-making process.

I found as a commander that my team performed best when they understood the *why* behind our mission. This philosophy falls in line with best-selling author and visionary thinker Simon Sinek's ideas on leadership. In his book, *Start with Why: How Great Leaders Inspire Everyone to Take Action*, Sinek asserts that people won't truly buy into a product, service, movement, or idea until they understand the *why* behind it.[1] This approach may seem counterintuitive to a military organization where we are known for following orders, but I found that if I could provide the intent behind what we were doing, my team performed better because they had buy-in or at least understood the purpose behind the task they were given. There are times in the military, often in combat, where subordinates need to follow orders without question, but I would argue that most of the time, understanding intent results in greater effort from the team, increased buy-in, and elevated desire to succeed.

STARTING WITH WHY

Regardless of the type of organization we lead, communicating a clear commander's intent ensures the team has a clearly understood common purpose. It helps individuals and teams alike understand how they fit into the larger operation or mission. Sinek goes on to say that we should start by explaining the *why* behind what we do so we can connect our team with a common purpose. If we are aligned toward a common purpose and goal and understand the roles we each play in achieving that goal, then we can work together to elevate the performance of our team.

In Operation Iraqi Freedom, when we got the briefing that A-10s would be doing close air support in downtown Baghdad, we knew there would be significant threats to our aircraft. Baghdad was surrounded by what we called the Super MEZ or missile engagement zone. We called it a Super MEZ because multiple overlapping missile engagement zones surrounded the city, meaning we would be targeted by multiple missile sites if we entered the airspace over Baghdad. We believed there would be significant air defenses that we would either have to take out or battle our way through to support our ground troops. Despite the threat and the risks, we knew this was a mission we needed to do. We believed in the mission of supporting our troops on the ground. If they were going to Baghdad, then we would be right there with them. We were aligned toward a common purpose, and we understood our roles. This was our reason for being and our reason for action.

CONSIDERATIONS FOR LEADERS

In any organization, civilian or military, a team needs to understand the *why* behind what they are doing so it gives them purpose. How can you ensure your team knows your intent and feels empowered to act?

- Explain the reasons for goals, missions, policies, and procedures in an organization.
- Encourage team members to ask questions and seek clarification as required.
- Share decision-making rationale. This enables team members to better understand your thought process.
- Embolden team members to make decisions and move out once they understand your intent.

A clear commander's intent ensures the team can adapt and make real-time decisions. And in the absence of a leader's direction and guidance, a team can take advantage of fleeting opportunities. When we share our thinking, it enables us to delegate and empower our subordinate leaders to make their own decisions and act in critical moments. It takes courage to trust our team and to empower them to act. *If you want to lead with courage, then share your commander's intent and enable your team to seize fleeting opportunities.*

EPILOGUE: CALL TO ACTION

"It is not the critic who counts; not the man who points out how the strong man stumbles, or where the doer of deeds could have done them better. The credit belongs to the man who is actually in the arena, whose face is marred by dust and sweat and blood; who strives valiantly; who errs, who comes short again and again, because there is no effort without error and shortcoming; but who does actually strive to do the deeds; who knows the great enthusiasms, the great devotions; who spends himself in a worthy cause; who at the best knows in the end the triumph of high achievement, and who at the worst, if he fails, at least fails while daring greatly, so that his place shall never be with those cold and timid souls who neither know victory nor defeat."

—Theodore Roosevelt

FINDING MY "WHY"

One day after flying a close air support mission in Iraq in 2003, I came back to the operations building to find a note from a group of soldiers who had stopped by to see me. The note, scribbled on a piece of paper, simply said, "Thank you. You saved our ass."

That note meant more to me than anything else. I didn't need anything more than that. I loved my job and the mission and people we were tasked to support. For me, it was all about service to our troops on the ground and helping them get home safely. I had found my purpose and my passion.

Simon Sinek talks about the importance of this concept in his follow-on book, *Find Your Why: A Practical Guide for Discovering Purpose for You and Your Team*. As Sinek explains, the WHY is the purpose, cause, or belief that drives every one of us. Sinek goes on to explain that "every single one of us is entitled to feel fulfilled by the work we do, to wake up feeling inspired to go to work, to feel safe when we're there and to return home with a sense that we contributed to something larger than ourselves."[1]

183

Figure E.1 With my family after my final flight in the A-10. My boys took part in the tradition of hosing me down after the flight, but weren't as excited about taking the picture.
Photo credit: Airman First Class Giovanni Sims.

One afternoon after we returned from deployment, we were all told to report to the main briefing room for a commander's call. Pilots, maintenance, and support personnel filled the seats with standing room only in the back of the large auditorium. As it turned out, I was going to receive the Distinguished Flying Cross for Heroism for my actions in Iraq. I certainly didn't feel like a hero, especially knowing all the heroic pilots who had come before me who had earned this distinction.

According to the Air Force Personnel Center, the Distinguished Flying Cross, authorized by an Act of Congress on July 2, 1926, was awarded first to Captain Charles A. Lindbergh, of the US Army Corps Reserve, for his solo flight of 3,600 miles across the Atlantic Ocean in 1927. The medal is awarded to any officer or enlisted person of the armed forces of the United States for heroism or extraordinary achievement while participating in aerial flight. Both heroism and achievement must be entirely distinctive, involving operations that are not routine. The V device is worn on decorations to denote valor, an act or acts of heroism by an individual above what is normally expected while engaged in direct combat with an enemy of the United States, or an opposing foreign or armed force, with exposure to enemy hostilities and personal risk.

I stood at attention facing the men and women of the 23rd Fighter Group as the narrator read the citation for my Distinguished Flying Cross:

The President of the United States of America, authorized by Act of Congress, July 2, 1926, takes pleasure in presenting the Distinguished Flying Cross with Combat "V" to Captain Kim N. Campbell, United States Air Force, for heroism while participating in aerial flight as an A/OA-10 fighter pilot, 75th Expeditionary Fighter Squadron, 332d Expeditionary Operations Group, 332d Air Expeditionary Wing at Ahmed Al Jaber Air Base, Kuwait on 7 April 2003. On that date, at North Baghdad Bridge, Iraq, flying as Yard 06, Captain Campbell's professional skill and airmanship directly contributed to the successful close air support of ground forces from the 3d Infantry Division and recovery of an A-10 with heavy battle damage. While ingressing her original target area, Captain Campbell was diverted to a troops-in-contact situation where enemy forces had positioned themselves within 400 meters of the advancing friendly forces and were successfully preventing the lead elements of the 3d Infantry Division from crossing the North Baghdad Bridge. Unable to eliminate the enemy without severe losses, the ground forward air controller had requested immediate close air support. After a quick situation update and target area study, Captain Campbell expertly employed 2.75-inch-high explosive rockets on the enemy position that had been threatening the advancing forces, scoring a direct hit, and silencing the opposition. During her recovery from the weapons delivery pass, a surface-to-air missile impacted the tail of Captain Campbell's aircraft. Immediately taking corrective action, she isolated the hydraulic systems and placed the A-10 into the manual reversion flight control mode of flight and prepared for the long and tenuous return flight to Kuwait. Captain Campbell's aviation prowess and coolness under pressure directly contributed to the successful completion of the critical mission and recovery of a valuable combat aircraft. The outstanding heroism and selfless devotion to duty displayed by Captain Campbell reflect great credit upon herself and the United States Air Force.

As the narrator finished reading the citation, I turned to face the 4th Fighter Wing Commander, Brigadier General Eric Rosborg, and stood at attention as he clipped the Distinguished Flying Cross medal to the nametag on my flight suit. I saluted then turned back to face the men and women of the 23rd Fighter Group. Did I really earn this? Was I worthy of this distinction when so many pilots had performed under pressure and saved the lives of our ground troops during our time in Iraq?

Don't get me wrong, I was enormously honored to receive the Distinguished Flying Cross for my actions in Iraq, but honestly, the most important and meaningful recognition came from our troops on the ground. From a note of thanks scribbled on a paper to a word of thanks from a soldier with tears in his eyes—those moments meant more to me than anything else. More recently, I received a note from a daughter whose father had been on the ground in Iraq.

> I know that without your aid that day a lot more of his men would not have come home. So, for all of us that were lucky enough to have our loved ones live another day thanks to your actions—Thank You.

That note reminded me of my "why." I never really thought I would stay in the Air Force as long as I did. Initially, I just wanted to be a fighter pilot. But while flying the A-10, I found my "why." I was so committed to supporting our troops on the ground that I was willing to risk my life for them. That mission was bigger and more important than me alone.

FINDING YOUR "WHY"

When I talk to cadets or new officers who are preparing for pilot training, I often talk about the importance of finding your "why." My advice to them is that they pick an airplane to fly based on the mission. Is it important for them to pick the latest and greatest, shiny, new airplane or to select an airplane with a mission that appeals to them? The A-10 certainly wasn't shiny or new; it's called the Warthog for a reason, but I connected with its mission of supporting our troops on the ground.

As I've moved into the next chapter of my life, I've realized the same advice still applies. *Do I want to pick a job based on the money I will make or the satisfaction that comes with the work?* Don't get me wrong, it's nice to have both, but if I have to choose one over the other, I've realized how important it is to have job satisfaction—to find purpose and meaning for what you do.

After my final flight in the A-10 in 2018, I had to find my new "why"— what was my purpose? I would find it at the Air Force Academy. My "why" became all about giving back and helping to teach and mentor the next generation of leaders.

Not long after hitting send on my retirement application, I sent an email to the Commandant of Cadets at the Air Force Academy letting her know I was retiring and moving to Colorado. We had met once before at the Pentagon, but I wanted her to know I was available to work with cadets in any capacity that might be of assistance. She immediately asked me to call her. She wanted to know if I would reconsider my retirement to come back to the Academy. She needed rated officers at the Academy to help mentor cadets. She also wanted my husband to consider the offer as well. Scott and I talked about the decision and thought it would be an effective way to continue serving while also having more stability in our family life. I loved the idea; it would be a way for me to give back and continue serving.

A few months later, we both got word we had assignments to the Academy. We didn't believe it would be possible until we saw it in writing. I was assigned to serve with the Dean of Faculty in the Department of Military and Strategic Studies, and Scott was assigned to be the Vice Commandant of Cadets. We were excited to go back to the Academy, to be able to mentor cadets and share our lessons learned with them.

COMING FULL CIRCLE

I pulled up to the gate at the Air Force Academy, almost 21 years after I had graduated. So far, it all looked the same, only this time, the gate guard saluted me and said, "Welcome back to the Academy, ma'am."

I made my way up to the cadet area, a drive I made on my first day of basic cadet training. I parked at the base of the ramp, formerly known as the Bring Me Men ramp, but now known as the Core Values ramp. Instead of Bring Me Men, the ramp was emblazoned with the words: Integrity First, Service Before Self, and Excellence in All We Do. In 2003, Air Force leaders decided that the poetic reference Bring Me Men was out of step with the current Air Force culture and offensive to many people. I personally never had an issue with it; the words were from a poem, but

I also understood the decision to replace the words with a new statement more reflective of the values of our Air Force and Air Force Academy.

It was exciting to be back. I loved everything the institution stood for — to educate, train, and inspire men and women to become leaders of character, motivated to lead the Department of the Air Force in service to our nation. I couldn't wait to be part of it all again. After all these years, I didn't think about the hardships or the struggles, I just remembered the good times, the friends I made, the pride in being here with a mission to serve. I was hoping to impart some of the things I had learned along the way in my career to cadets who would soon replace me.

I was nervous for my first day of class but excited, too. This was a recurring feeling throughout my career, a sense of nervousness mixed with excitement about a new adventure. I had taught pilots how to fly, so I knew something about being an instructor, but teaching in the classroom was an all-new experience. I wanted the cadets to be excited about learning. My goal was always to help them understand how what they were learning in the classroom would also apply to their time in the Air Force (and now, also the Space Force).

It turns out that cadets today are not all that different from when I was at the Academy as a cadet. Cadets have the same struggles with time management, staying awake in class, and trying to be good at military, athletic, and academic endeavors. They are still excited about the future and are driven to serve their country. It was rewarding and energizing to be around them.

My classroom certainly looked a little different than it did in 1997 when I was a cadet. According to the Air Force Academy, the Class of 2020 included 281 women (29% of the class, a significant increase from the 16% when I was there). The class also included 296 minority cadets (Asian, Hispanic, African American, Pacific Islander, and Native American), which was 30% of the class (compared to just 19% in 1997). It was nice to know that some things had changed for the better, but other things had stayed the same, such as the belief in core values of integrity, service, and excellence, as well as a commitment to serve our country in a time of war. I was proud of my cadets and excited for their opportunities ahead.

I was offered the opportunity to fly down at the airfield in the mighty T-53, also known as the Cirrus SR 20. The T-53s represent the backbone of the Academy's powered flight training program in which over 500 cadets participate annually. The powered flight program provides the foundation for the personal and professional discipline required to succeed as an Air Force aviator. My job was to introduce cadets to powered flight. I even got to solo a few of them. It was exciting and nerve-wracking as I got out of the airplane, watched them start and taxi away, hoping all would go well. Some were confident and some were nervous, but I had confidence in all of them, or I wouldn't have let them go solo. I missed flying the A-10, but it was rewarding to see how excited the cadets were about flying an airplane, many for the first time. It was rewarding to know that in some way I had helped prepare the next generation of Air Force officers and pilots.

My new "why" was all about serving the next generation of leaders, helping them to grow and learn the importance of service to something bigger and more important than themselves. I was passionate about giving back to the institution that had given so much to me. I found passion and purpose for what I was doing. But was it enough?

LIFE-CHANGING DECISIONS

After two years at the Air Force Academy, I once again faced a critical decision. Would I stay on active duty a few more years or elect to retire? As much as I loved my time with cadets, I was ready to depart. More important, my family was ready. I wanted and needed to spend more time with my family, and I was eager to start thinking about life's next adventure. And so, once again, I submitted my retirement application, but this time with confidence that the timing was right.

The last few months of my time on active duty did not go as expected. When the global pandemic hit, we went to online teaching at the Academy. Graduation moved up to April instead of May. We also stopped flying with cadets, though that didn't stop my interaction with the cadets I cared so much about. They had a lot going on and I wanted to be available to them as much as possible as they made their transition to the operational Air Force as second lieutenants. I enjoyed my online classes with them as we transitioned from our traditional coursework to discussions about life after the Academy.

The day before graduation, cadet squadrons held commissioning ceremonies where they took the oath of office and pinned on their lieutenant bars, just as we had 23 years ago. Two of the cadet squadrons asked if I would be their guest speaker for their ceremonies. I was honored and humbled to be part of those ceremonies, especially since friends and family were unable to attend due to the pandemic. All of the ceremonies would happen virtually and were live streamed to family and friends around the world. As I put on my mess dress for what I thought was the last time, I was flooded with a wave of memories from my time in the Air Force. Then as I put on my face mask, required for wear on military bases due to the threat of COVID-19, I was reminded that this was a time like no other. I never imagined a face mask would be part of my mess dress uniform.

I also got the opportunity to commission one of my students and administer the oath of office. It was heartwarming to watch these ceremonies, and it gave me confidence and hope in the future of the Air Force. My husband and I also shared the stage as guest speakers at one of the commissioning ceremonies, likely one of our last official functions before retirement. As I drove off the Academy grounds that night, I stopped at the scenic overlook that looks down on the cadet area. The sun was setting, the mountains were glowing in the background, and I was hit with a wave of emotion of how much this place meant to me. So many memories, challenges, and opportunities. I was thankful this was my path. There was no greater job or responsibility than service to this nation.

As I watched the graduation ceremony the next day on April 18, 2020, I was filled with pride for the cadets who had endured so much and were graduating in a time of crisis, not a traditional war, but still one that would create a unique set of challenges for these new second lieutenants. As I watched the cadets march onto the terrazzo and take the oath of office, it gave me time to reflect on my career and remember where it all started for me. More than anything, I am thankful for my friends and classmates who got me through those challenging times at the Academy.

My decision to retire was made easier knowing that these graduating cadets will very adequately follow in my footsteps.

NEEDS OF THE AIR FORCE

One evening, I was blissfully thinking about retirement, anticipating having more time at home, not having to be on someone else's schedule, and starting to plan for life after retirement, when I got a call from the Dean of the Faculty at the Academy. It was about 10 days before I officially out-processed from the Air Force, but I was still closing out a project for the dean, so I suspected she had a few questions for me. I was standing in our living room watching my kids play in the front yard, when I heard her ask, "So I know you're planning to retire soon, but . . . would you consider staying for another year?"

What? Her question caught me completely off guard, and my initial response was something like, "Hell no, I'm retiring!" My husband quickly looked over at me, wondering what we could be discussing. Thankfully, I had known the dean since we were cadets together, so my response to the one-star general officer wasn't completely out of line, although I quickly tried to throw in a "ma'am" at the end, so it didn't sound too bad. I was completely in shock. Here I was thinking about summer vacations (as much as we could think about vacations during a pandemic), and this was not what I expected at all. She told me I could take some time to think about it. The superintendent wanted to know if I would be willing to talk to him about a one-year extension to serve as the director of the Center for Character and Leadership Development. I had the weekend to think about it.

As I hung up the phone and looked over at my husband, he just laughed and said, "What now?!"

Seriously, if there was one job in the Air Force that could convince me to stay for another year, this would be it. I was passionate about mentoring cadets and being able to help them develop their character and leadership in preparation for service to the nation . . . how do you say no to that?

I talked to my parents. I talked to my husband. And I talked to my 11-year-old son. After explaining the job to him, he said, "Mom, it sounds like a good job. You should take it." With one caveat, he wanted to make sure that it was only for one year and that I would be available for all the vacation plans the next summer. I agreed.

I talked to the superintendent on Monday, and he walked me through what he was asking me to do. They had a gap in the director position, and he was asking me to stay on for one year until they could bring in a new director. I wanted to make sure I wasn't just keeping the lights on and the building warm, so I confirmed with him I would have the authority to make improvements to set the Center up for success for the next director. He wanted me to lead and make the needed changes. This wasn't just holding down the fort until someone else arrived.

I decided to take the job. I knew I could make a difference, that I could make an impact on the future of our nation's next generation of leaders in one more year of service. I was excited for the new role and the trust given me to develop our cadets and staff. It turns out, I also got the opportunity to develop myself. I had the privilege to learn from some of the best experts in character and leadership development. Over the year at the Center, they would teach me new things, give me new ideas, and help me grow. Leaders must always be willing to learn. At every level as leaders, we should strive to keep developing, just as we expect our people to do.

After my year as director ended, I stayed committed to the promise I had given my family. Retiring after 24 years of service was still tough, but I was ready.

After every career move or life-changing decision, it's natural to discover a new "why," a new purpose, and a new passion. Do I miss flying the A-10 and supporting our troops on the ground? Absolutely. But I found a new "why" in serving the next generation of leaders when I went back to the Air Force Academy. And now that I'm retired, I have a new passion and purpose . . . sharing the lessons learned. From war stories to life stories, we have a responsibility to share what we've learned so that others can grow, too.

When we find passion in what we do, we are more likely to put effort into it. Then the work doesn't feel like work, and we enjoy what we do. If you haven't yet found your "why," there's still time. Go find your purpose, go find your passion. It's worth it.

Figure E.2 Scott and I held a joint retirement ceremony at the Air Force Academy. As part of the ceremony, we pinned retirement pins on each other, signifying more than 49 years of combined military service. Photo credit: Justin R. Pacheco.

LEADING WITH COURAGE

As a young Air Force Academy cadet, I never imagined all the opportunities and challenges that I would have during my 24-year Air Force career. I never knew when I was going to be called on to execute at my highest level. The key is being prepared to confront fear and seize the moment.

Leaders are responsible for creating a culture in which being brave in the face of fear is expected. Why? Because when we act in the face of fear, we demonstrate both vulnerability and courage, and that paves the way for the trust that is necessary for high-performing teams. Leadership takes courage. It takes courage to show the human side of leadership, to have hard conversations, to make tough choices, to trust the members of our team, and to hold ourselves and others accountable. The practice of leadership isn't easy, and in moments of anxiety, stress, or fear, we need brave leaders who will lead with courage.

1. Turn into the wind. Have confidence that you can tackle the challenges that come your way.
2. Create a wingman culture in your organization.
3. Adopt a fighter pilot mindset and learn to fail forward.
4. Do the work. Be prepared to respond and adjust when the mission (or life) doesn't go as planned.
5. Be calm in the chaos. Your team is watching to see how you will respond.
6. Trust your team and empower your wingmen.
7. Take ownership of your actions and create a culture where mistakes and failures are opportunities for improvement.
8. Aviate, navigate, and communicate. Learn to prioritize under pressure and focus on what's most important first.
9. Bring clarity and confidence in the face of uncertainty. Recognize, confirm, recover.
10. Show the human side of leadership. Take the time to build connections with your team.
11. Create your own flight plan. Only you can choose the path that is right for you.
12. Share your commander's intent and enable your team to seize fleeting opportunities.

If you want to lead with courage, then fly in the face of fear. It's
what you do when you are scared that matters.

FROM USAFA TO BAGHDAD AND BEYOND

My mission over Baghdad was extremely challenging; it was also a defining moment for me. It pushed me to my limits and showed me what I was
capable of doing. That mission demonstrated to me the importance of
being prepared to seize the moment . . . that I could be decisive and act,
even when there was extreme risk involved and I was afraid.

During that mission, I experienced what I would explain as three distinct types of fear, and my response was different each time. First, there
was the immediate fear, when everything happened so fast that I barely
had time to think about it; I just reacted. When I was plunging toward
the ground over Baghdad, I was terrified. But I didn't have a lot of time
to think about it; I just had to react. Next for me was the calculated fear.
It came when I knew I was scared, stressed, and anxious (and I had too
much time to think about it). The flight back from Baghdad was grueling,
both mentally and physically. The decision to try to land or eject felt overwhelming at times, and I had what seemed like too much time to think
about it, to worry about the decision I needed to make. Finally, I faced
the fear of living with the decision. I was scared about what was going to
happen when I attempted to land my heavily damaged airplane, but at the
same time, I was confident in my decision.

These days, I'm not flying the A-10, but I still experience these distinct
types of fear. These may not be life-and-death situations anymore, but
they don't have to be. Like anyone, I get scared, fearful, or anxious, and
my body doesn't know the difference We can perceive an enemy shooting
at us *and* being put on the spot in a briefing as threatening. Although completely different types of threats (one life-threatening, the other pressure
and worry), experts tell us that our bodies activate a similar stress response.

A stressful situation, whether it's a life-or-death experience, a high-stakes
presentation, or a difficult conversation with a teammate or coworker . . .
all these situations can trigger stress hormones that produce physiological
changes. We've all had stressful moments where our heart starts pounding
and our breathing accelerates. We might even start sweating and notice
that our muscles feel tense. That's fear; that's stress. But these feelings are

also a survival mechanism. They help us react when we are faced with stress. Our body's response to stress can help us face fear and act in adverse and unexpected situations.

The goal is not to eliminate fear. Rather, it is key to acknowledge fear, anxiety, and stress and face it directly. We can find ways to harness the stress and adrenaline rush to improve our situation. Learn how to use it. Learn how to harness fear to your advantage. We all face fear in our lives. It's what we do when we are scared that matters.

As I look back on my career, I recognize that there were many times I was scared and had to work up the courage to face my fears. Whether it was walking up the Bring Me Men ramp as a basic cadet at the Air Force Academy, or walking into my fighter squadron on day one, or taking off in my A-10 to fly a risky close air support mission, or dropping my husband off for his one-year deployment to Afghanistan. In each of those situations, I felt fear. I wanted to do well, to prove myself, to perform at the highest level, and I knew it wasn't going to be easy. The thing is, facing fear isn't supposed to be easy. It can be a struggle. It can be hard. But in the end, we will be stronger for it. When we learn to overcome our fears, we open ourselves up to greater possibilities and we can seize opportunities.

I often think back to the conversation in the chow hall after my mission over Baghdad. Naturally, I wish I knew then what I know now. If I had to do it all over again, I would do it completely differently.

"So, were you scared?"

It still feels like everyone in the room is listening and waiting for me to answer. But now, instead of simply claiming I didn't have time to be scared, I own the feeling because I know what's important.

Was I scared? How could I NOT be scared?

Of course, I was scared. You can't have courage without fear. It's what you do when you are scared that matters.

What scares you? How are you going to embrace the fear and lead with courage? How will your courage change the trajectory of your life and those you lead?

When we act with courage, then our team is likely to do the same. And when we lead with courage, then we create an environment in which our team can excel.

ACKNOWLEDGMENTS

To the men and women I have served with, thank you for the honor of serving alongside you. Thank you for helping me to become a better person and leader. I owe tremendous praise and appreciation to my family, teachers, coaches, and friends who have influenced and supported me along the way. Thank you also to the many people who were gracious with their time and shared their experiences and lessons learned with me during this writing and publishing process. Thank you to my agent, Greg Johnson of the WordServe Literary Agency, who believed in me and this book. Thank you to my editor, Sunnye Collins, for providing invaluable input and making this book come alive. Thank you to Sally Baker, Debbie Schindlar, and the Wiley Team—you made this process fun and enjoyable. To my friends Casey Witman Sankey and Abigail Manning, who read the book in the initial stages, thank you for providing honest feedback and improving this book. I am forever grateful to my parents who have always believed in me and supported me, and to my brother, Alex, who is never afraid to give me an honest assessment. Finally, a special thanks to my husband, Scott, for always being by my side, listening in times of doubt, and supporting me along the way. And to my boys, Colin and Brodie, thank you for reminding me daily to focus on what's most important first.

NOTES

PROLOGUE

1. Brené Brown, *Dare to Lead* (New York: Random House, 2018), 3–6.

CHAPTER 1

1. Angela Duckworth, "What Is Grit?" accessed January 3, 2022, https://angeladuckworth.com/qa/#faq-125.

2. Angela Duckworth, *Grit: The Power of Passion and Perseverance* (New York: Scribner, 2016), 245.

CHAPTER 2

1. Air Force Handbook 1, *Airman*, November 1, 2021, 463.

2. Angela Duckworth, *Grit: The Power of Passion and Perseverance* (New York: Scribner), 244.

CHAPTER 3

1. Carol Dweck, *Mindset: The New Psychology of Success* (New York: Penguin Random House, 2016), 7.

2. Dweck, *Mindset*, 33.

3. Jim Mattis and Bing West, *Call Sign Chaos* (New York: Random House, 2019), 45.

CHAPTER 4

1. William L. Smallwood, *Warthog: Flying the A-10 in the Gulf War* (Washington: Brassey's, Inc., 1995), 11–12.

2. Smallwood, *Warthog*, 10.

3. Air Force Doctrine Publication 3–03, *Counterland Operations*, October 21, 2020, 8.

4. Anders Ericsson, *Peak: Secrets from the New Science of Expertise* (New York: Mariner Books, 2016), 62.

5. Carl Molesworth, *Sharks Over China: The 23rd Fighter Group in World War II* (Washington: Brassey's, 1999).

6. Clifton B. Parker, "Embracing Stress Is More Important Than Reducing Stress," *Stanford News*, May 7, 2015, https://news.stanford.edu/2015/05/07/stress-embrace-mcgonigal-050715/.

CHAPTER 5

1. Clifton B. Parker, "Embracing Stress Is More Important Than Reducing Stress," *Stanford News*, May 7, 2015, https://news.stanford.edu/2015/05/07/stress-embrace-mcgonigal-050715/.

2. Rebecca Grant, "An Air War Like No Other," *Air & Space Forces Magazine*, November 1, 2002, https://www.airforcemag.com/article/1102airwar/.

CHAPTER 6

1. "Iraq War," *Encyclopedia Britannica*, August 18, 2022, https://www.britannica.com/event/Iraq-War.

2. "Iraq War."

3. David Zucchino, *Thunder Run: The Armored Strike to Capture Baghdad* (New York: Grove Press, 2004).

4. Thomas H. Gray, *Manual Reversion Flight Control System for A-10 Aircraft*, March 1982, https://apps.dtic.mil/dtic/tr/fulltext/u2/a113463.pdf.

5. Mary Collins, "How Things Work: Ejection Seats," *Air & Space Magazine*, July 2002, https://www.airspacemag.com/military-aviation/how-things-work-ejection-seats-29088450/?page=2.

6. Kevin Bonsor, "How Ejection Seats Work," *How Stuff Works*, accessed January 3, 2022, https://science.howstuffworks.com/transport/flight/modern/ejection-seat.htm.

CHAPTER 7

1. Jim Mattis and Bing West, *Call Sign Chaos* (New York: Random House, 2019), 106.

CHAPTER 8

1. *Aircraft Accident Report: Eastern Air Lines, Inc.* (Washington, DC: National Transportation Safety Board, 1973).

CHAPTER 9

1. FAA Aviation Safety, "Spatial Disorientation," accessed January 3, 2022, https://www.faa.gov/news/safety_briefing/2016/media/SE_Topic_16–05.pdf.

CHAPTER 10

1. Amy J. C. Cuddy, Matthew Kohut, and John Neffinger, "Connect, Then Lead," *Harvard Business Review,* July–August 2013, https://hbr.org/2013/07/connect-then-lead.

CHAPTER 11

1. Department of Defense, *2020 Demographics Profile of the Military Community,* https://download.militaryonesource.mil/12038/MOS/Reports/2020-demographics-report.pdf.

2. Nick Erwin, "Air Force Clarifies Policies for Pregnant Aircrew," Air Force, April 11, 2022, https://www.af.mil/News/Article-Display/Article/2996101/air-force-clarifies-policies-for-pregnant-aircrew/.

3. Maj. Gen. Charles W. Lyon and Lieutenant Colonel Andrew B. Stone, "Right-Sizing Airpower Command and Control for the Afghanistan Counterinsurgency," *Air and Space Power Journal* 25, no. 2 (Summer 2011): 11, https://apps.dtic.mil/sti/pdfs/ADA544355.pdf.

4. Luis Martinez, "Afghanistan War," *ABC News,* July 14, 2010, https://abcnews.go.com/Politics/us-wounded-toll-afghanistan-half-2010-matches-2009/story?id=11166836.

5. Kirsten M. Keller et al., *Addressing Barriers to Female Officer Retention in the Air Force* (Santa Monica, CA: RAND Corporation, 2018), vii, https://www.rand.org/pubs/research_reports/RR2073.html.

CHAPTER 12

1. Simon Sinek, *Start with Why: How Great Leaders Inspire Everyone to Take Action* (New York: Penguin Books, 2009).

EPILOGUE

1. Simon Sinek, *Find Your Why: A Practical Guide for Discovering Purpose for You and Your Team* (New York: Penguin Books, 2017), vii.

ABOUT THE AUTHOR

Kim "KC" Campbell is a retired colonel who served in the United States Air Force for more than 24 years as a fighter pilot and senior military leader. Her final assignment was as the director of the Center for Character and Leadership Development at the United States Air Force Academy. As a senior military leader, Kim led thousands of airmen both at home and abroad in deployed locations and enabled them to succeed in their missions. She has experience leading complex organizations and driving cultural change. Kim has flown 1,800 hours in the A-10 Warthog, including more than 100 combat missions protecting troops on the ground in both Iraq and Afghanistan. In 2003, Kim was awarded the Distinguished Flying Cross for Heroism after successfully recovering her battle-damaged airplane after an intense close air support mission in Baghdad. Since retiring from the Air Force, Kim has shared her inspirational story and lessons on leading with courage with business and corporate audiences as an executive coach and keynote speaker. Kim and her husband, Scott, live in Colorado with their two sons.

Connect and learn more at www.Kim-KC-Campbell.com.

INDEX

3rd Infantry Division, arrival, 92–93

75th Fighter Squadron/23rd Fighter Group, 59–60, 69–70, 122–124, 186 photos, 85f, 124f, 131f

355th Fighter Squadron, 157

355th Fighter Wing, 168

355th Operations Support Squadron, 141f, 142, 163

414th Combat Training Squadron, 62

422 Test and Evaluation Squadron (TES) mission, 46–48

455th Expeditionary Operations Group, 133

612th Air Base Squadron, 145, 147f

612th Theater Operations Group/474th Air Expeditionary Group, command, 114, 168, 175f, 178

A

A-10 Thunderbolt II (Warthog) damage, 100f design, 53–55 display, 112f, 113f flying, 53f, 57–58

testing, 46–48 training, 55

Accountability assuming, 29–30 leadership accountability, 113–116 organizational belief, fostering, 34 ownership, 107

Action plan, visualization, 61–62

Actions commander intent, 176–178 ownership, 193 positive impact, 16 prioritization, 124 reason, 181 responsibility, courage, 114 slower is faster, 79

Adrenaline, impact, 94

Adversity, overcoming, 15–16, 101

Afghanistan, deployment, 69–78, 76f, 122–124, 124f, 131–137, 131f, 133f

Aggressiveness, 43

Air Force needs, 190–192 out-processing, 190–191

Air Force Academy
  Admissions Office, entry (key), 8
  application process,
      extensiveness/
      intensiveness, 9
  appointment
    acceptance, 14
    rejection, 12–13
  arrival, 15
  Assault Course, 24
  attendance, goal, 7
  Bring Me Men, 14–15, 20, 29
  cadets
    numbers, decrease, 25
    training, 187–189
  Cadet Wing, leading, 19f
  cemetery, 158
  classes, 26
  classmates, 76f, 153f
  commissioning ceremonies,
      31, 189, 190
  correspondence,
      continuation, 13–14
  entry, effort, 8
  female cadets, entry (1976), 6
  graduation, 31–32, 32f
    ceremony, 190
  joining, desire, 7
  Leadership Reaction
      Course, 24
  Long Blue Line, 21, 31–32
  members, characteristics, 8–9
  oath of office, 22
  online instruction, 189
  parent's weekend, 29
  pilots, attendance, 6
  preparation, father assistance, 11
  recognition, challenge, 26–27
  Run to the Rock, 27
  Seven Basic Responses, 21
  Survival, Evasion, Resistance,
      and Escape (SERE),
      27–28
  wingman concept, importance,
      19, 32–33
Airsickness, commonness,
    38–39
Al Jaber Air Base, 86, 90
American Volunteer Group
    (Flying Tigers), 59–60
Andrus, Randy, 101f
Approachability, importance,
    141–142
Arbaugh, Dana, 9, 13
Armed forces, women
  exclusion, 6–7
  joining, reasons, 9–10
Army, support, 89
Aspin, Les, 40
Attention, importance, 94–95
Attitude, 43

B
Bagram Air Base, 71, 74, 77, 131
  alert mission, 177
Balance, finding, 169–170
Bárány chair, usage, 38–39
Bárány, Robert, 39
Basic Cadet Training (BCT),
    20–25
  accomplishment, 25
  phases, 23

Basic fighter maneuvers (BFM),
    learning, 43
Basic Surface Attack mission, 58
Battle Damage, control,
    94–95
Breathing, importance, 78–80
Briefing
    debriefing, 107–110, 107f
"Bring Me Men" ramp, 14–15, 20,
    29, 187, 195
Brown, Brené, xiv, 139
Bush, George W., 69, 85, 88

C
Cadet Honor Code, 23
Cadets
    Assault Course, 24
    Basic Cadet Training
        (BCT), 20–25
    class, changes, 188
    graduation, 31–32, 32f
    honor code, adoption, 25
    leading, challenge, 29–30
    mentoring, 191–192
    numbers, decrease, 25
    squadrons, commissioning
        ceremonies, 189–190
    teaching, 187–189
Cadet Wing Commander
    Cadet Wing, leading, 19f
    position, selection, 28–30
Calculated fear, 194
Call Sign Chaos (Mattis),
    48, 116
Calmness, importance,
    80–81

Candidate Fitness Test, 11
Capability, establish-
    ment, 112–113
Cause, impact, 183
Center for Character and
    Leadership Development,
    125, 191
Chair flying, 55–56
Challenger, explosion (1986),
    5–7
Challenges, facing, 63–64
Change (driving), intent
    (sharing), 179–181
Chaos, calm (importance), 193
Civil Air Patrol
    cadet, Cessna flight, 3f
    uniform/marching/
        inspections, 23
Close air support (CAS), 53–55
Cohen, William, 31
Columbus Air Force Base, 154
Combat
    aircraft, women (legal banning/
        lifting), 40
    mission (Afghanistan), 69f,
        121f, 178f
    mission (Iraq), 85f, 100f, 101f
    readiness, 73–76
Combat search and rescue
    (CSAR) mission, 70–71,
    110, 133–134
Coming American, The
    (Foss), 14–15
Command and General Staff
    College (CGSC), education
    requirements, 159

Commander
  action, intent, 176–178
  intent
    impact, 175, 179
    sharing, 193
Common purpose, alignment, 181
Communication, 193
  clarity/concision/correctness, 81,
    122, 125–126
  continuation, 124
  technology, usage, 161–162
Competence, importance, 56
Confidence, 163, 193
  instilling, 81
  preparation, impact, 61–62
Confirmation, importance,
    135–138
Conflicts of interest, 168
Contingencies, planning, 63, 65
Control
  importance, 3, 94
  influence, contrast, 126–127
  maintenance, 97–98, 121
Controllability check, 97–98
Counterintuitiveness, 181
Courage
  impact, 114, 179
  usage, 193–194
Creative solutions, obtaining, 180
Creativity, increase, 144
Credibility, importance, 141–142
Crew chiefs, 57, 101, 132
Crisis, leadership, 125–126
Criticism, importance, 63
Cross-check, importance, 157
Cross-country race, 10–12, 12f

Cuddy, Amy, 144
Culture change, impact, 107

D
Data, study/review (importance),
    61–62
Davis-Monthan Air Force Base,
    142, 160, 164, 168
  A-10 training, 55–58
Debriefing, 107–110, 107f
Decision making
  empowerment, 101–102
  rationale, sharing, 182
Delegation, 127, 182
Deployment (difficulty), 161
Detail, importance, 23
Devil's advocate, 63
Discipline, importance, 23
Disorientation/visual cues
    (absence), 134–135
Distinguished Flying Cross for
    Heroism, 184–186
Distractions, impact, 123–124
Dollar ride, 39–40
Dream
  accomplishment, 3
  extension, 6–7
Drowley, Mike, 141–142
Duckworth, Angela, 16, 126
Dweck, Carol, 45

E
Education
  Command and General Staff
    College (CGSC), education
    requirements, 159

senior developmental education
(SDE), 164
Efficiency, increase, 157
Ego
exposure, 146
reduction, 149
Eielson Air Force Base,
157–158
Emergency procedures
evaluations, 37–38
sequence, adherence
(importance), 78–80
Emotions, reduction, 111
Empowerment, 102
intent, impact, 178–179
Engagement, rules, 71
Ericsson, Anders, 56
Events, facing, 4–5
Excellence in All We Do, 187
Exhaustion, 90, 97
Experiences
learning, 45, 144, 148
sharing, 167

F
Failing forward
learning, 193
mindset, 45–46
Failures, 48
fear, 37
improvement opportunities,
193
positive aspects, highlighting,
49
Family, 166f
assistance, 161

promise, 192
timing, 159–160
Fear
elimination, impossibility
(goal), 195
feelings, normalcy, 73
reduction, 94
types, responses, 194
Feedback, 30, 63, 113–114
honesty, 163
request, 116
trust, 114–115
Female role model, 166–167
Fighter pilot
becoming, 7
call signs, 39, 60, 61f
culture, 44
Introduction to Fighter
Fundamentals (IFF), 43–45
mindset, adoption, 193
Find Your Why (Sinek), 183
Fixed mindset, impact, 45–46
Flying (flight)
A-10 flights, 41–43, 46–48, 184f
A-10 Thunderbolt II (Warthog),
53–55, 53f, 57–58
Cessna flight, 3f
danger, 157
debriefing, 107–110, 107f
excitement, 188–189
exhaustion, 97
exhilaration, 5
flight plan, creation, 193
learning, 3–4
T-37 flights, 38–39
T-38 flights, 39–41, 37f

Focus, maintenance, 125–126
Follow-on assignments,
    examination, 168
Forward operating base (FOB),
    arrival, 77
Forward operating locations
    (FOLs), 179–180
Foss, Sam Walter, 14
Franks, Tommy, 75
Friends, support (importance),
    162
Fulfillment, importance, 170

G
Goals
    reasons, explanation, 182
    setting, 6
Grace, importance, 171
Grit (Duckworth), 16, 127
Growth mindset, shift, 46

H
Headwinds
    facing, 8–9
    obstacles, overcoming, 4–5
Help, request (realization),
    165–166
Henderson, Warren, 133
Heroism, distinctiveness, 184–185
Humanitarian mission, 132–133
Humility, importance, 141–142

I
Immediate fear, 194
Improvised explosive devices
    (IEDs), usage (increase),
    76–77

Influence, control (contrast),
    126–127
Information, obtaining, 177
Infrastructure, destruction
    (avoidance), 176
Innovation, importance, 144
Integrity First, 187
Intent
    action, commander intent,
        176–178
    impact, 175, 178–179
    sharing, 179–181
    understanding, 103
International Security
    Assistance Force (ISAF),
    augmentation, 160–162
Interviews, process, 166–167
Introduction to Fighter
    Fundamentals (IFF),
    43–45

J
Jobs
    change, 191–192
    dislike, 169
    love, 183
    satisfaction, 187
    selection, reasons, 186–187

K
Kennett, Nancy, 9–10
"Killer Chick" (KC) call sign,
    60, 61f

L
Leaders
    decisions, impact, 115–116

disciplined initiative,
    exercising, 175
mistakes, making, 113–114
motivation, 102
priorities, competition, 124
responsibility, ownership, 108
role, importance, 80–81
Leadership
    accountability, 113–116
    courage, usage, 193–194
    crisis, leadership, 125–126
    failure, 116
    human side, 142–144
    journey, mistakes/failure, 48
    problem, attention
        (importance), 115–116
    recognition/confirmation/
        recovery, 137, 138
    Red Flag leadership,
        62–64
    skills, learning, 24
    vulnerable leadership,
        challenge, 146–147
Learning, excitement, 188
Lessons learned, sharing
    (importance), 45
Life
    commitment, 5
    defining, 112–113
    demands, 154
    disconnection, 156–157
    facing, fear, 194
    life-changing decisions,
        189–190
    management, 163
    passion, 192
    risk, 25

Life-and-death situations/
    experience, 194–195
Lindbergh, Charles A., 184
Long Blue Line, 21, 31–32
Lorenz, Stephen, 30

M
Manual reversion, training/
    usage, 95–97
Mattis, Jim, 48, 115
McAuliffe, Christa, 6
McGonigal, Kelly, 62, 73
Meaning, finding, 187
Mentoring, 191–192
    session, 115
Micro-level tactical decision
    making, 46
Military customs/courtesies,
    basics, 23
Military hierarchy, learning, 21
Military joint doctrine, 175
Military training, mental/physical
    challenges, 10
Mission, 177, 181
    achievement, 63
    adjustment, 156, 193
    challenge, 194
    changes, adaptation, 77–78
    execution, importance, 116
    importance, 143
    objectives, discussion, 107
    planning, 87
    reasons, explanation, 182
    understanding, 103
Mistakes
    admission, 116
    allowance, 103

Mistakes (*Continued*)
  improvement opportunities,
    193
  making, 48, 113
  positive aspects, highlighting, 49
Morace, Ian, 101f
Motherhood, challenge, 165
Mutual support, 155

N
Nellis Air Force Base, 422 Test and
    Evaluation Squadron (TES)
    mission, 46–48
New Psychology of Success, The
    (Dweck), 45

O
Oath of office (Air Force
    Academy), 22
Objectives, debriefing, 108
O'Dowd, Mike, 69f, 71
Deployment (difficulty), 161
Officer's Club (O-Club),
    assignment night,
    42–43
Olds, Robin, 43
Operation Desert Storm, 45, 71,
    75, 96, 99
Operation Enduring Freedom,
    71, 131f, 162
Operation Iraqi Freedom, 80,
    86–100, 110, 181
Operations Group Commander,
    responsibility, 114–115
Operation Southern
    Watch, 70–71, 87

Opportunities
  pursuit, 170
  seize, 193
Organization, wingman culture
    (creation), 193

P
Patton, George, 176
Peak (Ericsson), 56
Peers, leading (challenge),
    29–30
Performance
  analysis, intentionality, 49
  importance, 60
  pressure, 39–40, 71–73
  reports, 163
Perseverance, 4, 10, 16
Personal information, sharing
    (impact), 159–160
Personal/professional challenges,
    navigation, 168, 170
Personal-professional life,
    balance (achievement),
    169–170
Perspectives, differences
    (learning), 164
Physical Fitness Test,
    requirements, 12
Pilots
  ejection, risks, 96
  skills, demands, 95
Pilot training
  A-10 selection, 41–43
  graduation, 42f
  first flights, 38
  formation flying, 41–42

ground training, 38
Officer's Club (O-Club),
    assignment night, 42–43
performance, pressure, 39–40
T-37 flights, 38–39
T-38 flights, 39–41, 37f
women, admittance, 40
Planning
  caution, 170
  discussion, 89–90
  importance, 64
Policies/procedures
  reasons, explanation, 182
Policies/procedures,
    differences, 179
Pope Air Force Base, 59–60
Power women, 9–10
Practice, importance, 56, 65
Pregnancy, 159–160
Preparation
  goal, 62–63
  importance, 61–65
Pressure, prioritization
    (learning), 193
Priorities
  competition, 124
  focus, maintenance, 125–126
  realization, 155
Prioritization, 81, 171
  concepts, 126–127
  effectiveness, 121–122
Professional military education
    (PME), 159
Purpose
  finding, 187
  impact, 183

Q
Questions, answering, 167
Questions, asking, 147–148
  fear, 148
  importance, 63
  team member questions, 182
Quitting
  avoidance, 16
  effects, 15

R
Randolph Air Force Base,
    Introduction to Fighter
    Fundamentals (IFF),
    43–45
Reactions, control, 80
Reconnaissance, usage, 90
Red Flag, 62–64
Rejection, pain, 15
Relationships, building, 149
Resilience, 4, 16, 22
Resnik, Judith, 6
Response, preparation, 193
Responsibility, 135
  leader ownership, 108
Retirement, 187, 191–192
  ceremony, 192f
Risk, 181
  aversion, 48
  embracing, 46–48
  openness, 149
  presence, 157–158
  reason, 5
  reduction, 126
Robinson, Lisa, 30
Roles, visualization, 63

Rosborg, Eric, 186
Rules/regulations,
        impact, 131–132

S
Sanitor, Robert, 53
Saturday a.m. inspections
        (SAMIs), 30
Schedules, deconflicting,
        168–169
Scheer, Jonathan, 157–158
Schutzius, Donna, 31
Self-confidence, 43
Senior developmental
        education (SDE), 164
September 11 (2001)
        terrorist attack,
        58–59, 73, 85
Service Before Self, 187
Seven Basic Responses, 21
Sinek, Simon, 180–181, 183
Situation
    analysis, 80
    monitoring, 177–178
Situational awareness
    improvement, intent
        (impact), 175
    requirement, 122
Skype, usage, 161–162
Solo takeoff, thrill, 4
Solutions, determination, 47
Soto Cano Air Base, 145
Start with Why (Sinek), 180–181
Stress, 86, 90, 124, 194–195
    adaptation, 135
    empathy, 81

feelings, normalcy, 73
    response, 38
    simulation, 37–38
Sub-leaders, disciplined
        initiative (exercising), 175
Super missile engagement zone
        (Super MEZ), 181
Support
    importance, 70–76, 88, 162
    mutual support, 155
    providing, 93, 132–134
Survival (survivability),
        99, 109–110
Survival, Evasion, Resistance,
        and Escape (SERE),
        27–28
Sweet, Rob, 45

T

T-37 flights, 38–39
T-38 flights, 39–41, 37f
T-53 flights (Cirrus SR
        20), 188–189
Tactical level operations,
        focus, 179
Tactics, execution, 46
Tailwinds, benefit, 4–5
Takeoffs/landing, difficulty,
        157–158
Tasks, prioritization/
        delegation, 127
Teacher, motivation, 8
Team
    appreciation, 113–114
    common purpose, 181

confidence, 156
connection, 149
contact, importance, 137
creative solutions, 180
efforts, focus, 24
evolution, culture change
   (impact), 107
importance, 101–102
improvement, desire, 45
meeting, 179
morale/welfare, checking, 168
mutual support, providing,
   32–33
performance, 180–181
pressure, 180
situational awareness
   (improvement), intent
   (impact), 175
strength, importance, 33
stress, alleviation, 30
trust, 193
virtual meeting, 125
Teammates, inspiration, 49
Team members
   questions/decisions, 182
   roles/responsibilities,
      approach, 34
   stress, empathy, 81
   training, importance, 103
Teamwork
   importance, 23
   learning, 24
Technology, impact, 161–162
Terrorism, global war, 69–71
Tevebaugh, Carol, 4

Threats, 181
   limitations, 126
   study/discussions, 87–88
Time management
   difficulty, 26
   importance, 23
Trust, 102, 135, 146
   creation, 149
   environment, establishment,
      34, 116
   team, trust, 193
Turner, Rick, 92, 100f, 101

U
Uncertainty
   clarity/confidence, supply, 193
   openness, 149
Unexpected, facing, 135, 137
UN Security Council
   Resolution 1441, 85
Upside of Stress, The
   (McGonigal), 62, 73

V
Value, feeling (significance), 167
Vision, understanding, 103
Visual lookout responsibilities, 33
Vulnerability, embracing, 49,
   143–144, 149
Vulnerable leadership,
   challenge, 146–147

W
War, precipice, 85–86
Warthog (Sanitor), 53
What-if questions, asking, 63

Why, finding, 181, 183–187
Winds, adjustment, 4–5
Wingmen
  assistance, 121
  culture, creation, 193
  empowerment, 193
  importance, 19, 32–33, 77
  pairing, 87–88, 132, 177
  plan, discussion, 136
Work-life balance, 163–166,
  169–170
Wormuth, Christine, 166